Modern Critical Interpretations

Geoffrey Chaucer's
The Pardoner's Tale

Edited and with an introduction by

Harold Bloom
Sterling Professor of the Humanities
Yale University

Chelsea House Publishers ◊ 1988
NEW YORK ◊ NEW HAVEN ◊ PHILADELPHIA

Printed and bound in the United States of America

10 9 8 7 6 5 4 3 2 1

∞ The paper used in this publication meets the minimum
requirements of the American National Standard for
Permanence of Paper for Printed Library Materials, Z39.48–1984.

Library of Congress Cataloging-in-Publication Data
Geoffrey Chaucer's The pardoner's tale / edited and with an
    introduction by Harold Bloom.
        p.   cm. — (Modern critical interpretations)
    Bibliography: p.
    Includes index.
    Summary: A collection of nine critical essays on Chaucer's "The
Pardoner's Tale" arranged in chronological order of publication.
    ISBN 0–87754–906–0 (alk. paper) : $24.50
    1. Chaucer, Geoffrey, d. 1400. Pardoner's tale.   [1. Chaucer,
Geoffrey, d. 1400. Pardoner's tale.   2. English literature—History
and criticism.]   I. Bloom, Harold.   II. Series.
PR1868.P3G46 1988
821'.1—dc19   87–22193
                                                                      CIP
                                                                      AC

Contents

THIS IS PAGE v

Editor's Note

This book brings together a representative selection of the best modern critical interpretations of the Pardoner's Tale from Chaucer's *Canterbury Tales*. The critical essays are reprinted here in the chronological sequence of their original publication. I am grateful to Bruce Covey for his assistance in editing this volume.

My introduction meditates upon Chaucer as Shakespeare's truest precursor in the representation of moral and emotional change brought about by and in a figure such as the Pardoner, who reacts to what he himself has said. Ian Bishop begins the chronological sequence of criticism with a consideration of the twofold narrative art of the Pardoner's Tale, while Penelope Curtis demonstrates how the tale, more than any other, "articulates the hidden principle in its teller's nature."

In two brief but crucial exegeses, the late Donald R. Howard emphasizes the uncertainty of the manuscript text, and then questions the "naturalness" of the Host's fierce response to the Pardoner in the epilogue. Warren Ginsberg, treating the tale as "sermon," studies the old man as a figure of avarice, after which H. Marshall Leicester, Jr., gives an overview contrasting the Pardoner's explicit exegesis of his tale with Chaucer's implicit interpretation.

In Monica E. McAlpine's discussion, the significance of the Pardoner's supposed homosexuality is expounded, while Robert P. Merrix analyzes the structure of the sermon in the Pardoner's Tale. R. A. Shoaf, in this volume's final essay, reads the Pardoner's Tale as an instance of the New Testament assertion that the letter, or literal reading, kills.

Introduction

Chaucer is one of those great writers who defeat almost all criticism, an attribute he shares with Shakespeare, Cervantes, and Tolstoy. There are writers of similar magnitude—Dante, Milton, Words-worth, Proust—who provoke inspired commentary (amidst much more that is humdrum) but Chaucer, like his few peers, has such mimetic force that the critic is disarmed, and so is left either with nothing or with everything still to do. Much criticism devoted to Chaucer is merely historical, or even theological, as though Chaucer ought to be read as a supreme version of medieval Christianity. But I myself am not a Chaucer scholar, and so I write this introduction and edit this volume only as a general critic of literature, and as a common reader of Chaucer.

Together with Shakespeare and a handful of the greater novelists in English, Chaucer carries the language further into unthinkable triumphs of the representation of reality than ought to be possible. The Pardoner and the Wife of Bath, like Hamlet and Falstaff, call into question nearly every mode of criticism that is now fashionable. What sense does it make to speak of the Pardoner or the Wife of Bath as being only a structure of tropes, or to say that any tale they tell has suspended its referential aspect almost entirely? The most Chaucerian and best of all Chaucer critics, E. Talbot Donaldson, remarks of the General Prologue to the *Canterbury Tales* that:

> The extraordinary quality of the portraits is their vitality, the illusion that each gives the reader that the character being described is not a fiction but a person, so that it seems as if the poet has not created but merely recorded.

1

As a critical remark, this is the indispensable starting point for reading Chaucer, but contemporary modes of interpretation deny that such an illusion of vitality has any value. Last June, I walked through a park in Frankfurt, West Germany, with a good friend who is a leading French theorist of interpretation. I had been in Frankfurt to lecture on Freud; my friend had just arrived to give a talk on Joyce's *Ulysses*. As we walked, I remarked that Joyce's Leopold Bloom seemed to me the most sympathetic and affectionate person I had encountered in any fiction. My friend, annoyed and perplexed, replied that Poldy was *not* a person, and that my statement therefore was devoid of sense. Though not agreeing, I reflected silently that the difference between my friend and myself could not be reconciled by anything I could say. To him, *Ulysses* was not even persuasive rhetoric, but was a system of tropes. To me, it was above all else the personality of Poldy. My friend's deconstructionism, I again realized, was only another formalism, a very tough-minded and skeptical formalism. But all critical formalism reaches its limits rather quickly when fictions are strong enough. L. C. Knights famously insisted that Lady Macbeth's children were as meaningless a critical issue as the girlhood of Shakespeare's heroines, a view in which Knights followed E. E. Stoll who, whether he knew it or not, followed E. A. Poe. To Knights, Falstaff "is not a man, but a choric commentary." The paradox, though, is that this "choric commentary" is more vital than we are, which teaches us that Falstaff is neither trope nor commentary, but a representation of what a human being *might* be, if that person were even wittier than Oscar Wilde, and even more turbulently high-spirited than Zero Mostel. Falstaff, Poldy, the Wife of Bath: these are what Shelley called "forms more real than living man."

Immensely original authors (and they are not many) seem to have no precursors, and so seem to be children without parents. Shakespeare is the overwhelming instance, since he swallowed up his immediate precursor, Christopher Marlowe, whereas Chaucer charmingly claims fictive authorities while being immensely indebted to actual French and Italian writers and to Boccaccio in particular. Yet it may be that Chaucer is as much Shakespeare's great original as he was Spenser's. What is virtually without precedent in Shakespeare is that his characters *change themselves by pondering upon what they themselves say*. In Homer and the Bible and Dante, we do not find sea-changes in particular persons brought about by those persons' own language, that is, by the differences that individual diction and tone make as speech produces further speech. But the Pardoner and the Wife of Bath are well along the mimetic way that leads to Hamlet and Falstaff. What they say to others, and to themselves, partly reflects what they already are, but partly engenders also what they will be. And perhaps even more subtly and forcefully, Chaucer suggests ineluctable transformations going on in the Pardoner and the Wife of Bath through the effect of the language of the tales they choose to tell.

Something of this shared power of Chaucer and Shakespeare accounts for the failures of criticism to apprehend them, particularly when criticism is formalist, or too given over to the study of codes, conventions, and what is now called "language" but might more aptly be called applied linguistics, or even psycholinguistics. A critic addicted to what is now called the "priority of language over meaning" will not be much given to searching for meaning in persons, real or imagined. But persons, at once real *and* imagined, are the fundamental basis of the experiential art of Chaucer and Shakespeare. Chaucer and Shakespeare know, beyond knowing, the labyrinthine ways in which the individual self is always a picnic of selves. "The poets were there before me," Freud remarked, and perhaps Nietzsche ought to have remarked the same.

II

Talbot Donaldson rightly insists, against the patristic exegetes, that Chaucer was primarily a comic writer. This need never be qualified, if we also judge the Shakespeare of the two parts of *Henry the Fourth* to be an essentially comic writer, as well as Fielding, Dickens, and Joyce. "Comic writer" here means something very comprehensive, with the kind of "comedy" involved being more in the mode, say, of Balzac than that of Dante, deeply as Chaucer was indebted to Dante notwithstanding. If the Pardoner is fundamentally a comic figure, why then, so is Vautrin. Balzac's hallucinatory "realism," a cosmos in which every janitor is a genius, as Baudelaire remarked, has its affinities with the charged vitalism of Chaucer's fictive world. The most illuminating exegete of the General Prologue to the *Canterbury Tales* remains William Blake, whose affinities with Chaucer were profound. This is the Blake classed by Yeats, in *A Vision,* with Rabelais and Aretino; Blake as an heroic vitalist whose motto was "Exuberance is Beauty," which is an apt Chaucerian slogan also. I will grant that the Pardoner's is a negative exuberance, and yet Blake's remarks show us that the Wife of Bath's exuberance has its negative aspects also.

Comic writing so large and so profound hardly seems to admit a rule for literary criticism. Confronted by the Wife of Bath or Falstaff or the suprahumane Poldy, how shall the critic conceive her or his enterprise? What is there left to be done? I grimace to think of the Wife of Bath and Falstaff deconstructed, or of having their life-augmenting contradictions subjected to a Marxist critique. The Wife of Bath and difference (or even "differance")? Falstaff and surplus value? Poldy and the dogma that there is nothing outside the text? Hamlet and Lacan's Mirror Phase? The heroic, the vitalizing pathos of a fully human vision, brought about through a supermimesis not of essential nature, but of human possibility, demands a criticism more commensurate with its scope and its color. It is a matter of aesthetic tact, certainly, but as Oscar Wilde taught us, that makes it truly a moral matter as well. What devitalizes the Wife of Bath, or Falstaff, or Poldy, tends at last to reduce us also.

III

That a tradition of major poetry goes from Chaucer to Spenser and Milton and on through them to Blake and Wordsworth, Shelley and Keats, Browning and Tennyson, and Whitman, Yeats, and Stevens, D. H. Lawrence and Hart Crane, is now widely accepted as a critical truth. The myth of a Metaphysical countertradition, from Donne and Marvell through Dryden, Pope, and Byron on to Hopkins, Eliot, and Pound, has been dispelled and seen as the Eliotic invention it truly was. Shakespeare is too large for any tradition, and so is Chaucer. One can wonder if even the greatest novelists in the language—Richardson, Austen, George Eliot, Dickens, Henry James, and the Mark Twain of *Huckleberry Finn* (the one true rival to *Moby-Dick* and *Leaves of Grass* as *the* American book or Bible), or Conrad, Lawrence, and Faulkner in this century—can approach Shakespeare and Chaucer in the astonishing art of somehow creating fictions that are more human than we generally are. Criticism, perhaps permanently ruined by Aristotle's formalism, has had little hope of ever accurately describing this art. Aristophanes, Plato, and Longinus are apter models for a criticism more adequate to Chaucer and to Shakespeare. Attacking Euripides, Aristophanes, as it were, attacks Chaucer and Shakespeare in a true prolepsis, and Plato's war against Homer, his attack upon mimesis, prophesies an unwaged war upon Chaucer and Shakespeare. Homer and Euripides after all simply are not the mimetic scandal that is constituted by Chaucer and Shakespeare; the *inwardness* of the Pardoner and Hamlet is of a different order from that of Achilles and Medea. Freud himself does not catch up to Chaucer and Shakespeare; he gets as far as Montaigne and Rousseau, which indeed is a long journey into the interior. But the Pardoner *is* the interior and even Iago, even Goneril and Regan, Cornwall and Edmund, do not give us a fiercer sense of intolerable resonance on the way down and out. Donaldson subtly observes that "it is the Pardoner's particular tragedy that, except in church, every one can see through him at a glance." The profound phrase here is "except in church." What happens to, or better yet, *within* the Pardoner when he preaches in church? Is that not parallel to asking what happens within the dying Edmund when he murmurs, "Yet Edmund was beloved," and thus somehow is moved to make his belated, futile attempt to save Cordelia and Lear? Are there any critical codes or methods that could possibly help us to sort out the Pardoner's more-than-Dostoevskian intermixture of supernatural faith and preternatural chicanery? Will semiotics or even Lacanian psycholinguistics anatomize Edmund for us, let alone Regan?

Either we become experiential critics when we read Chaucer and Shakespeare, or in too clear a sense we never read them at all. "Experiential" here necessarily means humane observation both of others and of ourselves, which leads to testing such observations in every context that indisputably is relevant. Longinus is the ancestor of such experiential criticism, but its masters are Samuel Johnson, Hazlitt and Emerson, Ruskin, Pater, and Wilde. A century gone mad on method has given us no critics to match these, nor are they likely to come again soon, though we still have Northrop Frye and Kenneth Burke, their last legitimate descendants.

IV

Mad on method, we have turned to rhetoric, and so much so that the best of us, the late Paul de Man, all but urged us to identify literature with rhetoric, so that criticism perhaps would become again the rhetoric of rhetoric, rather than a Burkean rhetoric of motives, or a Fryean rhetoric of desires. Expounding the Nun's Priest's Tale, Talbot Donaldson points to "the enormous rhetorical elaboration of the telling" and is moved to a powerful insight into experiential criticism:

> Rhetoric here is regarded as the inadequate defense that mankind erects against an inscrutable reality; rhetoric enables man at best to regard himself as a being of heroic proportions—like Achilles, or like Chauntecleer—and at worst to maintain the last sad vestiges of his dignity (as a rooster Chauntecleer is carried in the fox's mouth, but as a hero he rides on his back), rhetoric enables man to find significance both in his desires and in his fate, and to pretend to himself that the universe takes him seriously. And rhetoric has a habit, too, of collapsing in the presence of simple common sense.

Yet rhetoric, as Donaldson implies, if it is Chaucer's rhetoric in particular, can be a life-enhancing as well as a life-protecting defense. Here is the heroic pathos of the Wife of Bath, enlarging existence even as she sums up its costs in one of those famous Chaucerian passages that herald Shakespearean exuberances to come:

> But Lord Crist, whan that it remembreth me
> Upon my youthe and on my jolitee,
> It tikleth me aboute myn herte roote—
> Unto this day it dooth myn herte boote
> That I have had my world as in my time.
> But age, allas, that al wol envenime,
> Hath me biraft my beautee and my pith—
> Lat go, farewel, the devel go therwith!
> The flour is goon, ther is namore to telle:
> The bren as I best can now moste I selle;
> But yit to be right merye wol I fonde.
> (WBP, ll. 475–85, E. T. Donaldson, 2d ed.)

The defense against time, so celebrated as a defiance of time's revenges, is the Wife's fierce assertion also of the will to live at whatever expense. Rhetorically, the center of the passage is in the famously immense reverberation of her great cry of exultation and loss, "That I have had my world as in my time," where the double "my" is decisive, yet the "have had" falls away in a further intimation of mortality. Like Falstaff, the Wife is a grand trope of pathos, of life defending itself against every convention that would throw us into death-in-life. Donaldson wisely warns us that "pathos, however, must not be allowed to carry the day," and points to the coarse vigor of the Wife's final benediction to the tale she has told:

> And Jesu Crist us sende
> Housbondes meeke, yonge, and fresshe abedde—
> And grace t'overbide hem that we wedde.
> And eek I praye Jesu shorte hir lives
> That nought wol be governed by hir wives,
> And olde and angry nigardes of dispence—
> God sende hem soone a verray pestilence!
>
> (*WBT*, ll. 402–8)

Blake feared the Wife of Bath because he saw in her what he called the Female Will incarnate. By the Female Will, Blake meant the will of the natural woman *or* the natural man, a prolepsis perhaps of Schopenhauer's rapacious Will to Live or Freud's "frontier concept" of the drive. Chaucer, I think, would not have quarreled with such an interpretation, but he would have scorned Blake's dread of the natural will or Schopenhauer's horror of its rapacity. Despite every attempt to assimilate him to a poetry of belief, Chaucer actually surpasses even Shakespeare as a celebrant of the natural heart, while like Shakespeare being beyond illusions concerning the merely natural. No great poet was less of a dualist than Chaucer was, and nothing makes poetry more difficult for critics, because all criticism is necessarily dualistic.

The consolation for critics and readers is that Chaucer and Shakespeare, Cervantes and Tolstoy, persuade us finally that everything remains to be done in the development of a criticism dynamic and comprehensive enough to represent such absolute writers without reduction or distortion. No codes or methods will advance the reading of Chaucer. The critic is thrown back upon herself or himself, and upon the necessity to become a vitalizing interpreter in the service of an art whose burden is only to carry more life forward into a time without boundaries.

V

Chaucer, writing at our American moment, would have written "The TV Evangelist's Tale," rather than "The Pardoner's Tale." Alas, we have no contemporary Chaucer to give us "The TV Evangelist's

Prologue" and "The TV Evangelist's Epilogue," for which so much superb material has been provided in recent revelations. That is the context, aside from all historicisms, old and new, in which Chaucer's Pardoner should be seen. He is at once obscenely formidable and a laughable charlatan, thus arousing in us ambivalences akin to those provoked by certain eminent preachers on our home screens.

In the General Prologue to the *Canterbury Tales* we first encounter the Pardoner as the Summoner's lustful companion, boisterously singing the tavern air, "Come hither, love, to me," and producing, with his Summoner friend, a sound surpassing the trumpet's cry. With his wax-like yellow hair, hanging like a lank of flax, thin and fine, and his piercing high voice, and his lack of beard, the Pardoner is the very type of the eunuch. We understand then why he hangs close to the authentically obscene Summoner, so as to pick up some sexual coloring, as it were. Beneath the overcompensation of lustful behavior, which fools nobody, the Pardoner is dangerously close to being an emblem of death, like the uncanny old man of his tale. The association of castration, blindness, and death, so crucial in Freud, is already a given in Chaucer, just as the strangely authentic power of the Pardoner's sermon, which transcends his overt tricksterism, testifies to the weird prolepsis of Dostoevsky in the *Canterbury Tales*. A professional hypocrite who yet can invoke the terror of eternity, truly despite himself, the Pardoner is the most powerful representation of depravity we can find in English before the creation of Shakespeare's Iago and Edmund. Even Talbot Donaldson underestimates, I think, the Pardoner's depth of self-destructiveness:

> But the Pardoner's secret is, of course, a secret only to himself: at any rate Chaucer the pilgrim guessed it at once. But as long as the secret remains unspoken the Pardoner dwells securely in his own delusion, so that the secret remains valid for him. Yet at the end of his frightening story he wantonly imperils—and destroys—the fragile structure on which his self-confidence depends. Whatever his reasons—avarice, good-fellowship, humor—he concludes his sermon with an offer to sell his pardon to the pilgrims even after all he has told about his own fraudulence. Ironically he picks the worst possible victim, that rough, manly man who might be supposed to have a natural antipathy for the unmasculine Pardoner. The insult to the Host's intelligence is the first and last failure of the

Pardoner's intelligence, for the Host's violently obscene reaction reveals the Pardoner's secret. Thereupon the man whose clever tongue has seemed to give him control of every situation is reduced to furious silence.

I do not think that "avarice, good-fellowship, humor" are the only reasons why the Pardoner so brazenly insults Harry Bailly, the most likely of all his listeners to give the brutal and inevitable riposte. Moved by the extraordinary intensity of his own tale-telling, the Pardoner achieves a kind of vertigo that mixes pride in his own swindling with something dangerously authentic out of the supernatural order of grace:

> O cursed sinne of alle cursednesse!
> O traitours homicide, O wikkednesse!
> O glotonye, luxure, and hasardrye!
> Thou blasphemour of Crist with vilainye
> And othes grete of usage and of pride!
> Allas, mankinde, how may it bitide
> That to thy Creatour which that thee wroughte,
> And with his precious herte blood thee boughte,
> Thou art so fals and so unkinde, allas?
> Now goode men, God foryive you youre trespas,
> And ware you fro the sinne of avarice:
> Myn holy pardon may you alle warice—
> So that ye offre nobles or sterlinges,
> Or elles silver brooches, spoones, ringes.
> Boweth your heed under this holy bulle!
> Cometh up, ye wives, offreth of youre wolle!
> Youre name I entre here in my rolle: anoon
> Into the blisse of hevene shul ye goon.
> I you assoile by myn heigh power—
> Ye that wol offre—as clene and eek as cleer
> As ye were born.—And lo, sires, thus I preche.
> And Jesu Crist that is oure soules leeche
> So graunte you his pardon to receive,
> For that is best—I wol you nat deceive.
>
> *(PT*, ll. 567–90)

A desperate good-fellowship and a kind of gallows humor certainly are present in those closing lines. What is also present is a sense that the Pardoner has been carried away, and by more than his tale's strength or his own rough eloquence as a preacher. A kind of

madness or enthusiasm takes possession of him and drives him to the
social suicide that Freud would have regarded as "moral mas-
ochism," the need for punishment due to an unconscious sense of
guilt, perhaps even a retroactive self-recognition that might account
for his emasculate condition. The drive for destruction again turns
inward and rages against the self, so that in courting a kind of social
death the Pardoner receives premonitions of the spiritual death he has
earned. That perhaps explains the outrageousness of the Pardoner's
address to his fellow-pilgrims:

> It is an honour to everich that is heer
> That ye mowe have a suffisant pardoner
> T'assoile you in contrees as ye ride,
> For aventures whiche that may bitide:
> Paraventure ther may falle oon or two
> Down of his hors and breke his nekke atwo;
> Looke which a suretee is it to you alle
> That I am in youre felaweshipe yfalle
> That may assoile you, bothe more and lasse,
> Whan that the soule shal fro the body passe.
> (*PT*, ll. 603–12)

What can the Pardoner have expected as response to this
outburst? The need for rebuke surely dominates the Pardoner's
address to the Host, which asks for more than trouble:

> I rede that oure Hoste shal biginne,
> For he is most envoluped in sinne.
> Com forth, sire Host, and offre first anoon,
> And thou shalt kisse the relikes everichoon,
> Ye, for a grote: unbokele anoon thy purs.
> (ll. 613–17)

The Host's splendidly violent response, with its images of
kissing the Pardoner's stained fundament and slicing off and carrying
away his testicles, is precisely what the Pardoner was too shrewd not
to expect. But the shrewdness here belongs to the Pardoner's
unconscious death drive; the merely conscious ego of the wretch is
stricken as silent as Iago was to be. Iago ends by saying that from this
time forth he never will speak a word. His true precursor, the
sublimely damned yet still comic Pardoner, also answered not a
word: "So wroth he was no word ne wolde he saye."

The Narrative Art
of the Pardoner's Tale

Ian Bishop

The Pardoner's Tale has often been praised for its dramatic irony, its concentration and the sense of awe that it engenders; it has more than once been described as one of the best short stories in English. The purpose of the present article is to reexamine some of the ways in which Chaucer achieves this result. I do not propose to do this by comparing the tale with its analogues—that has already been done by Mrs. Germaine Dempster among others. I shall rather compare some aspects of Chaucer's narrative technique in this tale with techniques that he employs in some of the most successful of his other short stories. But that is not my principal intent. My main purpose is to suggest that the concentration and the uncanny power of this tale are the result of three things in particular: a threefold economy, a double perspective and a unifying irony.

It is generally agreed that much of the tale's fascination is due to the figure of the "oold man and a povre" who directs the three rioters to the treasure. Yet there has been considerable disagreement about the identity and the significance of this character. In a recent article in *Medium Ævum,* however, John M. Steadman has offered an explanation of his function which is based more firmly upon Chaucer's text than are most of the other interpretations. According to Steadman the old man is not a sinister or a supernatural figure: he is neither the Wandering Jew nor Death in disguise. Moreover,

From *Medium Aevum* 36, no. 1 (1967). © 1967 by the Society for the Study of Mediaeval Languages and Literature.

although one of his functions is to act as a *memento mori,* he is not a personification of Elde, one of the traditional messengers of Death. On the other hand, Professor Steadman will not follow W. J. B. Owen to the position of extreme naturalism and argue that he "is an old man and nothing more." Whereas Owen maintains that the old man invents the story about Death being under the tree as a convenient means of getting rid of the drunkards who offer him violence, Steadman argues that, like the hermit in some of the tale's analogues, the old man really has seen the treasure and, in his wisdom, has passed it by because he "knows the causal relations between cupidity and death." Steadman regards the old man as a generalized "notion of aged humanity" and aptly remarks that Chaucer's "attempt to delineate the general through the particular brings him close to the frontiers of allegory, but he does not actually cross." The way in which this generalized figure hovers near the frontiers of naturalism and of other modes of presentation is one of the factors that produce the double perspective which I shall discuss later.

The present article is not concerned with the tale's prologue and epilogue or with the relationship between the tale and its teller; it is concerned almost exclusively with the story of "thise riotoures thre" as it is narrated between C. 661 and 894 (F. N. Robinson, 2d ed.). Nevertheless, before I proceed to an analysis of the tale proper, it is necessary to say something about the discourse on the sins of the tavern which separates the false start of the story at line 463 from its true beginning at line 661. What I have to say about this digression is so obvious that it would be hardly worth mentioning, were it not for the fact that it seems to have escaped the notice of several scholars who have written about this tale and who have offered some extravagant and cumbersome explanations of the presence of this passage.

The digression is, of course, entirely relevant to the *sentence* of the *exemplum* which it interrupts. Although Avarice is the radical sin that is illustrated in the tale, the three sins that are denounced in the digression—drunkenness, swearing and gambling—all contribute to the bringing about of the tale's catastrophe. If the rioters had not been drunk, they would not have set out upon their quest to "sleen this false traytour Deeth" in the first place. If they had not been so profligate with their oaths, they might have taken more seriously their covenant of brotherhood and might have paid more attention to the solemn, admonitory imprecations of the old man. "Hasardrye" is obviously related to Avarice, but it is perhaps worth remarking that the habitual desire of each of the revellers to play for the highest possible stakes causes him to plot against one or both of his "brothers" and so is directly responsible for inducing the internecine catastrophe.

Once the tale proper has begun there is no further interruption: the action moves forward with a relentless logic to what, when it is reached, appears to be the inevitable conclusion—given the rioters' characters and the circumstances in which they find themselves. This rapid, irresistible progression is reinforced by Chaucer's economy in narrative technique. Not only is there an absence of digression, but an economy in three things principally: in characterization, in description and in narrative itself. I shall consider each of these three in turn.

One of Chaucer's happiest methods of adapting his sources was to pay particular attention to distinctive details of characterization. This can be seen even in such a brief narrative as the Prioress's Tale, where the pathos is considerably enhanced by the way in which the "litel clergeon" is individualized, mainly through his conversation with his more mundane schoolfellow. In the Pardoner's Tale, however, individualization of character is kept to a minimum. The only character to be described in detail is the old man and, as we have already seen, he is a generalized figure, compounded of "commonplaces" that were traditionally associated with old age. He is sharply contrasted with the "riotoures thre," but they are themselves hardly individualized at all: any one of them could have played the part of any other. It might be argued that this is simply because they are presented as a trio of "sworn brothers," who speak and act in concert—"we thre been al ones" (l. 696)—until they come upon the gold. It might be pointed out in support of this argument that Aleyn and John, the cooperative pair of clerks in the Reeve's Tale, are far less easy to distinguish than are Nicholas and Absalom, the pair of rivals in the Miller's Tale, whose characters are so carefully contrasted.

The clerks in the Reeve's Tale, however, are distinguished at least by name; whereas in the Pardoner's Tale all the characters, whose voices we hear so clearly, remain anonymous. It is true that this is not the only tale in which the characters are anonymous: there is the Prioress's Tale, for example; but, as we have seen, the "litel clergeon" in that tale is endowed with a distinct personality of his own. What is so striking about the Pardoner's Tale is the combination of anonymity and impersonality. There is other evidence which suggests that this is deliberate on Chaucer's part. It is uncertain how much importance should be attached to the fact that names are given to the rioters' counterparts in some of the analogues. But it is surely undeniable that it would have been simpler and more convenient for Chaucer if he had referred to the various members of his trio by using personal names, instead of resorting to the slightly clumsy and obtrusively impersonal means of differentiation that we find in the tale: "the proudeste of the three," "the worste," "the yongeste," "the firste shrewe," "that oon," "that oother". . . . What seems to me to clinch the matter is the answer that the servant gives when one of the rioters bids him:

> "Go bet . . . and axe redily
> What cors is this that passeth heer forby;
> *And looke that thou reporte his name weel.*"
> (F. N. Robinson, 2d ed., ll. 667–69;
> italics mine)

But we no more learn the dead man's name than we learn the name of the servant himself—or, indeed, the names of the rioters, the taverner, the old man or the apothecary. The servant informs his master merely: "He was, pardee, an old felawe of youres." Three lines later, however, the intention behind all this contrived anonymity becomes clearer. The final line of the master's command has alerted us: we expect to hear a proper name; but the fulfilment of our expectations is delayed and transferred. Instead of hearing the name of the stricken man, we hear the name of his assailant: "Ther cam a privee theef men clepeth Deeth." This is the only proper name we hear—apart from the name of God—until we reach the final episode.

It is perhaps not too fanciful to argue that Death is the only "character" in the tale who is completely individualized and presented as a complex personality. We are shown several facets of his character: his capriciousness; the arbitrary way in which he strikes or refuses to strike; his stealth and elusiveness; the subtlety and irony of his way of working. We also encounter some of his "espye[s]" and those who are truly "of his assent": *not*—as one of the rioters and some modern critics allege—the old man; but plague and heart-attack, and—more pertinently—Drunkenness, Swearing, Gambling, and, above all, Avarice.

This "character study" is communicated to the reader through the dialogue and by means of implication. The only character who is described in detail is the old man, as we have seen, and that description is conveyed mainly through dialogue. In several of his tales Chaucer "amplifies" his matter by introducing his characters through more or less formal *effictiones,* but also by giving descriptions, either concentrated or dispersed, of the setting and background of the action. In the Pardoner's Tale, however, he is content with a bare minimum of stage properties, which are introduced to indicate a change of scene and to provide a concrete centre around which the characters can group themselves. The rioters meet the old man "as they wolde han troden over a stile." He tells them that, if they "turne up this croked wey," they will find Death under an oak. Nothing is seen of the funeral *cortège* at the beginning of the tale; the clinking of the bell is merely heard "offstage"—and, incidentally, is all the more alarming for being introduced in the very next couplet after the one in which we are told that the rioters were sitting in the tavern "Longe erst er prime rong of any belle." When Romeo wishes to buy "a dram of poison," Shakespeare indulges in an extended description of the apothecary's shop, but we are vouchsafed no description whatever of the establishment that the youngest rioter visits for his more venomous purpose. On the other hand, Chaucer reports in detail the false arguments that the rioter used to persuade the apothecary to sell him the poison, and then, modulating into *oratio recta,* he tells us precisely what the apothecary said in reply:

> "And thou shalt have
> A thyng that, also God my soule save,
> In al this world ther is no creature,
> That eten or dronken hath of this confiture
> Noght but the montance of a corn of whete,
> That he ne shal his lif anon forlete;
> Ye, sterve he shal, and that in lasse while
> Than thou wolt goon a paas nat but a mile,
> This poysoun is so strong and violent."

Chaucer's reporting this conversation in full, while remaining silent about the setting, brings me to the third kind of economy that is noticeable in this tale: what can only be called "economy of narrative." It has often been remarked that much of the tale consists of dialogue and that this is mainly responsible for its dramatic quality. But it has another consequence too: the fact that we so seldom hear the narrator speaking *in propria persona* means that plain narrative, when it does occur, is all the more arresting and telling. Before the full effect of this economy can be properly examined, however, it is necessary to observe just how much information about character, motive, and circumstance Chaucer manages to convey through almost completely unannotated dialogue.

The very first exchange sets the pace for the whole tale and subtly introduces two of its most disquieting features. We hear the master's peremptory "Go bet," but his servant does not obey. There is no need for the serving-boy to leave the tavern in order to satisfy the rioter's inquiry about the meaning of the lich-bell; he knows the answer already: "It was me toold er ye cam heer two houres" (l. 671). The uneasy sensation of having been anticipated—whether by another character, by events, or by unseen powers—increases as the tale proceeds. The other disturbing feature I have already touched upon: the rioter asks for the dead man's name, but the boy gives him instead the name of his sinister assailant. This is symptomatic of the essential movement of the plot: when the rioters expect to meet Death, they find the treasure; they find Death, "hwenne [hie] weneþ to libben best."

From the boy's speech it emerges that he conceives of death in the way that his mother had taught him to do, as a "privee theef" armed with a spear, who strikes men unexpectedly and goes stealthily on his way. Being but a child, he is not so sophisticated as to know about personification and allegory; he accepts as literally true what his mother had told him: " 'Thus taughte me my dame; I sey namoore.' " The taverner confirms what the boy has said about the activities of Death during the current epidemic of plague. He continues to speak of Death as if he were a real person, following the boy's remark; but he is, presumably, speaking figuratively, whereas the boy was not. Perhaps we are meant to think of him as humouring the boy—with an innkeeper's tact—by continuing to speak in his phrase; to have questioned his conception of Death would, after all, have meant flouting his mother's authority. For the rioters, who are thoroughly drunk by this time (l. 705), the distinction between literal and figurative meanings has become temporarily blurred. Having heard the boy speak of Death as if he were a real person, and then hearing the adult taverner do likewise, they are convinced that he is a palpable public enemy. So they form themselves into a company of "sworn brothers," like knights errant engaged on a dedicated quest, and resolve to seek out "this false traytour Deeth" and slay him. The resolution is made to the accompaniment of many great oaths.

When, in the next scene, they meet the old man, they continue to rend "Cristes blessed body" by their indiscriminate use of oaths. The old man, by contrast, is a courteous figure. He invokes the name of God only three times, and each time the invocation is solemn and deliberate. His last words to the rioters consist of such an invocation:

> "God save yow, that boghte agayn mankynde,
> And yow amende!" Thus seyde this olde man.

But the name of God has become so devalued in their mouths that it rings hollow in their ears. They are so impatient that they can hardly stay to hear the old man's words, let alone to heed them:

> "And yow amende!" Thus seyde this olde man;
> And everich of thise riotoures *ran*
> Til he cam to that tree.
>
> (ll. 767–69; italics mine)

Within the space of two lines of narrative they have been precipitated into the third scene and transported to the place where the catastrophe is to be played out. After only seven more lines of narrative dialogue is resumed.

The success of some of the best of Chaucer's shorter tales depends upon the way in which, during the final scene, events move towards their end with an astonishing rapidity and seeming inevitability. But the unimpeded flow of the action at the conclusion of these tales is often made possible only because the author has contrived to introduce into the earlier part of his narrative much of the information and most of the stage "properties" that are required for the enactment of the dénouement. This kind of anticipation is well illustrated in the Reeve's Tale, where the fact that the miller has a "piled skulle" is mentioned in the description of that formidable character with which the tale begins. A few lines later Chaucer smuggles in, by means of a parenthesis, a reference to the existence of the baby *and its cradle* at the moment when his principle purpose is to impress upon his audience the fact that—apart from this insignificant infant—the miller's daughter was his only child. The reader will be able to think of other examples without much difficulty. In the Pardoner's Tale Chaucer goes even further: all the technical details of the murders are conveyed to the reader in advance in the course of the dialogue between the two conspirators and in the account of the youngest rioter's visit to the village. So that when the moment for the catastrophe arrives, there is no need to describe the action in detail; the fate of the three "sworn brothers" is a foregone conclusion. It follows with an irresistible logic: the rioters are despatched without ceremony in ten lines of summary narrative that are delivered with the coolness and detachment of a mathematician spelling out the *quod erat demonstrandum* at the end of a theorem. The single couplet of misplaced exultation, uttered by one of the homicides, stands out in ironical relief in the middle of this passage where the narrator's own voice has now become dominant:

> What nedeth it to sermone of it moore?
> For right as they hadde cast his deeth bifoore,
> Right so they han hym slayn, and that anon.
> And whan that this was doon, thus spak that oon:
> "Now lat us sitte and drynke, and make us merie,
> And afterward we wol his body berie."
> And with that word it happed hym, par cas,
> To take the botel ther the poyson was,
> And drank, and yaf his felawe drynke also
> For which anon they storven bothe two.
>
> (ll. 879–88)

But the theorem has a corollary. Although the narrator refrains from giving a detailed description of the rioters' death, he does not allow us to forget the implications of the apothecary's words that I have already quoted. The apothecary had recommended his "confiture" to his customer by emphasizing the speediness of its action: it would kill any living thing in less time than it would take you to cover a mile at an ordinary walking pace. From the point of view of the writhing victims, however, twenty minutes is a very long time. Chaucer does not describe their death agony in a series of "close-ups" as Flaubert does when he recounts the death of Emma Bovary after she has taken poison. He prefers implication to description: he "distances" the scene and looks at it with the eyes of a coroner reading a pathologist's report that refers him to a standard medical textbook:

> But certes, I suppose that Avycen
> Wroot nevere in no canon, ne in no fen,
> Mo wonder signes of empoisonyng
> Than hadde thise wrecches two, er hir endyng.
>
> (ll. 889–92)

The educated contemporary of Chaucer would have recognized more readily than the modern reader just how much the narrator has deliberately left unsaid.

The peculiar strength of this tale derives not only from the kinds of economy and narrative skill that I have examined above, but also from the presence of a double perspective. Looked at in objective sobriety, all the events in the story can be accounted for rationally. We have already considered how the revellers came to set out on their mission to slay Death. The presence of the treasure under the tree may seem extraordinary, but there is no need to resort to supernatural explanations of how it came there. The old man is not portrayed "naturalistically": his characterization embodies too many of the commonplaces traditionally associated with aged humanity to satisfy the canons of *verismo* representation. But, as we have seen, it does not follow from this that he is, in fact, a supernatural being or an allegorical figure. Finally, the catastrophe can be explained in simple, psychological terms: the rioters bring their deaths upon themselves as the result of their habitual sins.

But we also see the action from another point of view. Much of the dialogue, of which the tale largely consists, is spoken by the revellers while they are drunk. Inebriation has an effect upon them not unlike that which sleep exerts upon the narrator of a mediæval "dream allegory": they are transported "In auenture þer meruayleʒ meuen"; we receive through their drunken eyes a glimpse of the world of "Fayerye." In that world the frontier between the realm of the marvellous and the realm of everyday experience is opened, so that denizens of the one may mingle freely with inhabitants of the other. It is an eclectic world in which giants and dragons live side by side with gods and demi-gods from various pantheons. Its origins have some associations with the Kingdom of Death (the classical underworld is easily metamorphosed into the fairy kingdom of *Sir Orfeo*); yet it harbours not only the shades of the departed, but also shadowy abstractions, personifications and allegorical figures. Death himself may be encountered walking abroad in this world with many of the attributes of a human being. Conversely, it is always possible that any human being one encounters there may, in fact, be a denizen of the "other realm," who has slipped across the frontier. When the rioters meet the strange figure "al forwrapped save [his] face," who seems to be too old to belong rightfully to the land of the living, they are at once suspicious and one of them accuses him of being Death's "espye" in league with him "to sleen us yonge folk." Because Chaucer's presentation of the old man hovers near the frontiers of allegory and personification, the rioter's allegations seem sufficiently plausible to make the reader wonder whether there may not be some substance to them. The fact that this nightmare world is nothing more than a drunken delusion does not diminish the disturbing effect that it has upon the atmosphere of the tale.

When the rioters find the treasure, they experience the sober certainty of waking bliss. The quest that they had embarked upon in their drunkenness is forgotten: the company of "sworn brothers" is no longer inspired by heroic intentions of ridding the world of a dangerous public enemy. In their sobriety their main source of inspiration is their avarice. As a direct result of their avarice they are destroyed; in their last game of "hasardrye," Death sweeps the board.

The two points of view from which the action is seen are brought into a single focus by means of an intertwining irony. The irony of the rioters' "finding Death" only after they have ceased to look for him is not original with Chaucer's version of the tale; but he develops it in a way that would appear to be his own. We have seen how, in the earlier part of the tale, Chaucer builds up the personality of Death, even to the extent of ensuring that he is the only "character" to be allowed a proper name. We have also noticed how, through the medium of the dialogue, he creates an atmosphere of mystery so that the reader has a sensation of being in the presence of uncanny "principalities and powers," in spite of the fact that the objective view of the action insists that this is all part of a drunken misapprehension. The dénouement reveals that "principalities and powers" are indeed present, but that Death is not the prime mover. In fact, death is seen in the event to be something quite negative; a thing without personality. We do not hear his hollow laughter at his moment of triumph. The spectre of Death vanishes from the rioters' minds as soon as they find the treasure, but one of them attributes their discovery of it to the benignity of another personified power,

Fortune (l. 779). She is the deity in whom these "hasardours" really believe, rather than the God whose name they are continually taking in vain. Later the malignant aspect of Fortune, of which the rioters are oblivious, is suggested by the context in which the phrase "par cas" occurs at line 885. Meanwhile the narrator indicates in passing (at l. 844) that the real power behind the scenes is neither Fortune nor Death, but "the feend, oure enemy" who is intent on trapping promising victims by means of their own sins. The rioters are as deluded in the world of sober calculation as they were in their drunken fantasy.

I remarked earlier that in the last game of "hasardrye" that the revellers play among themselves, Death steps in and sweeps the board. But Chaucer makes no such explicit comment. It would have been as inappropriate in the context as would any explicit reference to the "false traytour" or the "privee theef" with his spear. Nevertheless the naturalistic, objective narrative does happen to show, with tacit irony, how each of the rioters is slain by nothing other than a "privee theef" and a "false traytour"—his own "sworn brother." When the pardoner proceeds to his peroration, and points to the *sentence* of his *exemplum,* his theme is not the omnipotence of Death, but the sin of Homicide and the other sins whose "deadly" consequences are illustrated in the tale.

A further twist that Chaucer gives to the spiral of irony shows that he realized potentialities in the fable that would have appealed to a Greek tragedian; yet, at the same time, he in no way diminishes its propriety within the Christian ethos of his own day. When the rioters are about to set out on their quest, he causes them to boast in their drunkenness: "Deeth shal be deed." This piece of ὕβρις will sound to anyone acquainted with the Scriptures like a blasphemously materialistic application of St. Paul's promise that "Death shall be swallowed up in victory." It is therefore entirely fitting that when Νέμεσις follows it should afford a disturbingly *literal* illustration of another Pauline text: "the wages of sin is death."

The Pardoner's "Jape"

Penelope Curtis

The *Canterbury Tales* begins not only after the pilgrimage is ended but by rendering its end. It begins, that is, with the portrayal in the Prologue of a whole set of states and actions which are both present and yet, as the narrative describes them and the very tense of the verbs insists, already completed, perfected. The tense of the verbs is, appropriately enough, the "present-perfect"—appropriate, for this is one "ende" of pilgrimage, something actively aspiring, resonant, yet achieved. What is more, one may say of the General Prologue that the sequence of tenses moves from a completed act of retrospection towards a more excitable, ad hoc account of what the journey actually felt like. The imperfect tense ("whan that they were seeke") makes a breach in "Aprill" for the preterite tense—and so for the history of a journey and for the little prologues.

At the other "ende" of the poem the company is not seen to reach its destination. Instead, the Parson points a "weye" out of the poem altogether, directs the company, in his heavily didactic and aspiring prose, towards an ultimate Canterbury of the spirit. But between "Aprill" and the Sermon the meaning of the journey is tested by the pressures under which the company is placed: pressures from without, as with the advent of the Canon, or from within its own midst. Host and "peple" dominate the interrupted, semi-realistic journey; the narrator becomes their adept and invisible servant. What we call "living in the present" is more often living in

From *Critical Review* 11 (1968). © 1968 by Penelope Curtis.

the preterite, in the flash of immediate retrospect by which we recognize what has happened as an event. We live in such preterites in the prologues and the "wordes bitwene." These little prologues are highly, even fiercely, selective. They reveal an unusual, though inconstant, change of feelings and perceptions about the composition of the company and its purpose. Each is shaped as a dramatic episode; but I think that by far the most important, the most fully extended and imagined, and the one which most tests the depth of purpose in this seemingly "unfinished" and diverse work, is the Pardoner episode.

One is placed in immediate difficulties in dealing with the Pardoner. One wants to convey some sense of the almost hypnotically fluid power of his discourse, and yet also to show the hidden progression in his "pleye" which makes it so dangerous a "jape" in the company's life together. The poem offers to celebrate a holi-day, a journey, as a "game": a game of Tales and "pleye" and "japes." The Pardoner agrees first to tell a "jape," and then, under pressure from the people, to tell "som moral thyng" instead. In fact he tries to perpetrate his "moral thyng" as a highly ambitious, quite new kind of "jape" which, if it should succeed, would satisfy his rage against their common life and dissipate the whole "game," the common enterprise, in a fantasy of his own making. He tries to bring the company under the influence of his "bisynesse"; to change "thise gentils" whom he flatters as "Lordynges" into "lewed peple" and set them in his "chirches"; to make fools of them at their own festival, and, by setting up a makeshift booth for on-the-spot salvation, to make nonsense of any journey of aspiration to any Canterbury. He tries to dissolve their milieu, to suspend time, and to remake the very identity of his hearers: in other words, to annihilate the very terms in which the company and its journey are conceived. But the journey, the historic perspective, the common enterprise all survive him. His failure is brought about by the combined influences of the "peple" and their representatives, Host, Knight and narrator. Where he tries to trick Host and people out of their powers of memory, tries to make them realize his fantasy as well as reflect it, by assent of "wolle," the company reassert the past and reaffirm their purpose by an "oon assent" all the more powerful for his challenge. The shape of the Pardoner's "jape" is seen only in the glow of his defeat. To trace it, however cursorily, from "The wordes of the Hoost to the Phisicien and the Pardoner" to the swift little manoeuvre by which the narrator sets his attempt definitively in the past, one is forced to recognize this episodic shape as well as the anarchic powers released within it.

The Tale also defeats his attempt, of course: simply by detaching itself and all its meanings from the influence of his personality. If he had succeeded with it, if he had taken possession and made it work for *him,* he would have undermined and mocked that other great principle of the Host's "juggement": the autonomy of "the tale." As it is, there is no point of contact between his Tale and the surrounding discourse. The Pardoner disappears into the Tale, and his capacities of mind and spirit are so made over, so translated, that they do nothing to evoke his personality. His preaching is all personality-play: his Tale shows nothing of such play. He fails to possess his Tale, as it fails to convert him. Yet the opposition magnificently projects the opposition struggling in his being. He is so deeply, so bafflingly divided, that one may say he is committed to the double defeat, almost that he has chosen the one truly impossible task for his "jape": that of destroying what, for him, incontrovertibly *is*. His Tale is intimately and permanently bound to him in contradiction. No other tale is so surrounded and isolated by its teller's perfor-mance, even as that is isolated and surrounded by the "game." Certainly no other tale so articulates the hidden principle in its teller's nature. Without his Tale, we could scarcely begin to account for his extraordinary gifts nor for his desperation. Nevertheless, I should like to concentrate here less on the Tale than on the immensely rich and subtle art revealed in the apparently casual Prologue.

The first thing to notice is the way the whole Physician-Pardoner "Fragment" achieves a certain unity in depth. Virginia's cry, "Goode fader, shal I dye? / Is ther no grace, is ther no remedye?" receives two answers whose opposition might sum up the deep division between the Pardoner and his Tale: from himself a promise of endless grace and remedy—"So that ye offren, alwey newe and newe"—and from the Tale a mysterious silence, a pattern of mortality, and a hint that death itself may be remedy, the thing sought and pleaded for: "But yet to me she wol nat do that grace." However, the Physician's Tale belongs, with *The Legend of Good Women,* to a simpler, stiffer Chaucerian "rhetoric" than the headlong comedy which follows. Nothing in it quite justifies the Host's outburst. His excitement seems, rather, prophetic. It anticipates the stir the Pardoner causes. It takes us into a new region of the prologue-pilgrimage experience, charging the poetry with a newly explosive play of dead-serious and burlesque meanings.

> Oure Hooste gan to swere as he were wood;
> "Harrow!" quod he, "by nayles and by blood!
> .   .   .   .
> Algate this sely mayde is slayn, allas!
> .   .   .   .
> This is a pitous tale for to heere.
> But nathelees, passe over, is no fors.
> I pray to God so save thy gentil cors,
> And eek theyne urynals and thy jurdones,
> .   .   .   .
> But wel I woot thou doost myn herte to erme,
> That I almoost have caught a cardynacle.
> By corpus bones! but I have triacle,
> Or elles a draughte of moyste and corny ale,
> .   .   .   .
> Myn herte is lost for pitee of this mayde."
>   (F. N. Robinson, 2d ed.)

I do not know what, if anything, one makes of an echo from the Harrowing of Hell in at least one mystery cycle, where Satan addresses Christ as *bel ami*. Very strangely, so it may appear, the Host uses the same term to the Pardoner: " 'Thou beel amy, thou Pardoner,' he sayde, / 'Telle us som myrthe or japes right anon' "; and there *is* a sense in which the Host plays the *advocatus diaboli* in this incident. His outburst, his invitation almost to a pact, seems to stir up some opposition between the Pardoner and (it is suddenly this) the crowd. The Pardoner is set apart, by a series of little interpositions, "quod he," and by his bearing: he picks up certain of the Host's expressions, turns them, as it were, back on him, speaks with a peculiar deliberation that is insolence itself. In the impressionistic narrative the very "alestake" seem to materialize at his gesture.

> But right anon thise gentils gonne to crye,
> "Nay, lat hym telle us of no ribaudye!
> Telle us som moral thyng, that we may leere
> Som wit, and thanne wol we gladly heere."

We have never been so conscious of the company as now when, Langland-like, rising suddenly to communal self-consciousness, it

insists on its dignity as "thise gentils." The peculiar preterite, "Oure
Hooste gan to swere" is striking enough: "gonne to crye" is more
excited still. The tense is fairly common in Langland, rare in
Chaucer. In *Piers Plowman* it is associated with unstable forms of
vision and community, and the vivid sensation of being in their
midst. It is so here; the Host's turbulence has called out theirs.

He has initiated a struggle of wills, and the Pardoner redefines
his intention all the more coolly, marking out the line-pause in
fastidious distinction from the crowd's surging past one ("we may
leere / som wit").

> "I graunte, ywis," quod he, "but I moot thynke
> Upon som honest thyng while that I drynke."

He accepts his isolation, creates a kind of glittering aura for himself
in laying down the terms. He is committed to a form of honesty, for,
if the "jape" is to be profoundly, not superficially, successful, he
must put weapons of truth in their hands and see them used in a
common symbolic suicide. If he can bring them to their knees and
their purses to his feet he will have projected the contradiction in
himself as tyranny over them. He has pitted his false calm, his
hyperconsciousness against the unconscious moral instinct of the
crowd. I call this instinct "moral," but it might equally be regarded
as an instinct for communal survival.

From the beginning the Pardoner works in paradox and antithesis, distinguishing most carefully between the very things he is most
concerned to blur and compound.

> "Lordynges," quod he, "in chirches whan I preche,
> I peyne me to han an hauteyn speche,
> And rynge it out as round as gooth a belle,
> For I kan al by rote that I telle.
> My theme is alwey oon, and evere was—
> *Radix malorum est Cupiditas.*"

The antitheses are set up: the "Lordynges" and the "chirches" into
which he invites them; "I" and "me." "I peyne me" is exactly what
he does, frivolously and at depth. Even in the fever of performance
"I" holds "me" up so insistently as an *object* of attention that the
words seem to take on properties of "he" and "him." Already as he
shocks and soothes us in that curiously blended tone which is
peculiar to him he begins his strange self-disengagement. It works

partly through his air of intimacy with what are as yet two very distinct audiences, in appraisal of the object ("me"), partly by his power of endowing that object, in its metaphoric forms, with an intense and separate life *out* of his own: "And rynge it out as round as gooth a belle." The whole prologue is a drawn out mingling of address and struggle, in which the vivid torment of "I peyne me" distracts our attention, while the "Lordynges" are being converted, by a kind of conjuring trick, into "lewed peple" and set in pews. He attempts to turn his fantasy about them into fact, and busily manipulates his entirely real spiritual suffering to do so. "My theme is alwey oon, and evere was": for a moment the line hangs poised between what goes before, "I preche," "I peyne," "I kan," "I telle," and what comes after. *"Radix malorum est Cupiditas."* No doubt he is offering himself as a live "ensample." Certainly his "theme" comprehends himself and himself talking. He is also presenting himself in another, even more dramatic light: he makes "confessioun" before the "peple." Example is a powerful weapon.

As he begins to imitate himself, to perform his performance, he gives us a self-portrait which rivals the best portraits in the General Prologue.

> "I stonde lyk a clerk in my pulpet,
> And when the lewed peple is doun yset,
> I preche so as ye han herd bifoore,
> And telle an hundred false japes moore.
> Thanne peyne I me to streeche forth the nekke,
> And est and west upon the peple I bekke,
> As dooth a dowve sittynge on a berne.
> Myne handes and my tonge goon so yerne
> That it is joye to se my bisynesse."

He mimes his own action, sees it isolated and dominant from the "peple's" position, shows it restless for escape in metaphor. The dove is a superb image, a parody of the "spirit" which moves him and whose innocence he derides, but also a perfect fluttering figure for his dissociation from his self, even from his body: neck, hands and tongue. The Wife of Bath gave us an unplaced image of a past self, "Gat-tothed I was, and that bicam me weel"; but the Pardoner can produce his "lost" self like a dazzlingly sarcastic credential. He can *make* that self as we watch.

Two features of the portrait may help account for the peculiar effect which their presence has in the General Prologue: a use of straining animal images to suggest a state of rebellion against nature, and a prevailing animus, a malevolent sarcasm. But the Pardoner sets their "object" in a place of high prominence, a place of power. His birdlike visibility is the condition of his sermon, utterly different from the Parson's where all sense of time and place is blotted out. Without his role, the Pardoner has no title, almost no being; and for him, to improvise a self is to summon up setting and congregation. In the bewilderment which follows, as he opens his motives more and more bafflingly, one almost looks round to the walls of his "chirches" as to the familiar. "If any *wight* be *in this chirche now*": the emphases are seductive; only, if one submits to that impulse, one sees only one figure, ever-present, ever-active in the throes of his power.

There is something frighteningly compulsive in his performance: the comparison that comes to mind is the Duke's in "My Last Duchess." But the Duke's reenactment of an inner drama is as coldly inexplicit as it is forced from him by passion; his performance is a social one, his satisfaction, his sense of release almost solitary. All the Pardoner's mimic-dialogues, however, develop his dependence on the real company for some ultimate sign of submission or assent. Even here, the performer's exultation is infused with a curiously undirected though self-analytic malice—"That it is joye to se my bisynesse"—which might be compared with the narrator's outburst at the climax of the Canon's appearance in the Canon's Yeoman's Prologue: "But it was joye for to seen hym swete!" The Pardoner's "joye" is self-consuming. It is partly the torment of doubleness, the conscious nervous play of then and now, there and here, performer and critic, this "joye" which makes the things distinguished live in one another, that mark his "confessioun" off from the most sophisticated figures of allegory. This prologue is an assault. The further he proceeds, the more committed he becomes to it *as* an assault, on common standards and language and on the company which has these things in its keeping:

> For myn entente is nat but for to wynne,
> And nothyng for correccioun of synne.
> I rekke nevere, whan that they been beryed,
> Though that hir soules goon a-blakeberyed!
>
> . . . .

> For whan I dar noon oother weyes debate,
> Thanne wol I stynge hym with my tonge smerte
> In prechying, so that he shall nat asterte
> To been defamed falsly, if that he
> Hath trespased to my bretheren or to me.
>
> . . . .
>
> Thus quyte I folk that doon us displesances;
> Thus spitte I out my venym under hewe
> Of hoolynesse, to semen hooly and trewe.

He is too articulate. The more he talks, the more he mocks speech as a power for truth or falsehood. The deeper he leads us into his contradictory motivation (its animus is directed inwards and outwards at once) the more it baffles us, and tricks us out of the very judgment with which his flatteries credit us. We are left with an exercise of power for unguessable motives. Whatever he means by "avarice," it cannot rest with what money can buy, unless money can buy damnation; our one poetic certainty is that he trades in that.

Dylan Thomas uses a similar image for an afterlife, where "Plenty as blackberries . . . / The dead grow for His joy"; but he *plants* his dead souls in Nature-simple. The surprise is a vivacious but naive one. Chaucer's "soules" are conceived in neither so unorthodox nor so secure a way. Whether errant or lost, at play or in torment, they move in inaccessible regions of the Pardoner's mind, shockingly dismissed to these by the crude pun. The shock comes not from the mysterious metaphor alone, nor from the man's hard heart, but from their concurrence. The metaphysical opposition is internalized in the one voice. Metaphors which dissociate "Myn handes and my tonge" from the speaker do not replace or blot out his personality, as Elde did the Reeve, but form an inseparable part of a personal action:

> Than ne wol I stynge hym with my tonge smerte
>
> . . . .
>
> Thus spitte I out my venym under hewe
> Of hoolynesse, to semen hooly and trewe.

The Pardoner's revelations, the "I" he announces, derive from and triumph over the Langland tradition. Chaucer has raised it from one stage of dramatic likelihood to another, from the "confession" made by the Summoner for the Friar, to those made for the Wife by her enemy-sex and for the Canon by "his" Yeoman. In the Pardoner at last we have "confession" for its own perverse sake, fully internalized as a struggle of powers in one man. It is more shocking a contradiction than, say, that of Langland's Sloth, for Sloth is roused out of silence and supported by a literary convention, whereas the Pardoner's confession has its own momentum of opposition. It is held together by extreme psychological tension, and directed towards a highly plausible, doomed, unprecedented, dramatic end.

At last it is the voice that carries a condition as nearly absolute as we will find: the condition of "I wol nat" and "I wol." The simplest facts replace metaphor as a focus for sheer will:

> "I wol nat do no labour with myne handes,
>
> . . . .
>
> I wol noon of the apostles countrefete;
> I wol have moneie, wolle, chese, and whete."

"Myne handes" are no longer actors, lively accomplices, but members which express and obey. The rebellious parts have been brought, by sheer spiritual intensity, under the supreme power "I wol nat do."

Our attention is wholly taken up with the self-portrait, the self-imitation; at the same time, the more sophisticatedly he invites us to see and judge him, the more our memory of who and where *we* are is blurred and superseded. I say "we" because the poem's audience and the Pardoner's audience are not distinct at this point.

> "First I pronounce . . ."
> "Thanne shewe I forth my longe cristal stones . . ."
> " 'Goode men,' I seye, 'taak of my wordes keep . . .' "
> "And, sires, also . . ."
> "Goode men and wommen, o thyng warne I yow . . ."
> "By this gaude have I wonne, yeer by yeer . . ."
> "But shortly myn entente I wol devyse . . ."
> "Thanne telle I hem . . ."
> "What, trowe ye . . . ?"
> "Nay, nay, I thoghte it nevere, trewely!"

The more subtly he discriminates between "ye" and "hem" (and the play of bullying and cajolery does not always follow the distinction) the more his tones insinuate the way one audience may be brought under the focus of another. The main effect of his syntactical subtleties is to undermine our sense of situation while seeming always to recall it. From seeing his "bisynesse" in the pulpit we are brought to a closer focus on his inner state, and scarcely notice how busily he retains and reactivates the assumptions, verbal gestures, tones of power, he used first to amuse us from his height. They have been internalized but by no means lost. He takes liberties with his "gentil" audience towards the end of the Prologue which he would not have risked at the beginning: "What, trowe ye?" for example, or "Now hoold your pees! my tale I wol bigynne." He does not yet begin the Tale at all, but by now we are in any case dependent on him. It is he who recalls us to a sense (however falsely deployed) of time and place. The cool gathering-in of terms, the feint at decorum, are part of the ambitious "jape."

The Tale appears to contain the Sermon; it seems a clear case of a sermon in parenthesis, an "exemplum." He has announced "my tale," and given it a time-honoured beginning, "In Flaundres whilom was a compaignye." But this is not the tale, nor the company of pilgrims, nor the "riotours" we meet later. It is more like a crowd of phantasmagoria.

> In Flaundres whilom was a compaignye
> Of yonge folk that haunteden folye,
> As riot, hasard, stywes, and tavernes,
> Where as with harpes, lutes, and gyternes,
> They daunce and pleyen at dees bothe day and nyght,
> And eten also and drynken over hir myght,
> Thurgh which they doon the devel sacrifise
> Withinne that develes temple, in cursed wise,
> By superfluytee abhomynable.

This is certainly not the Tale, it is a new sermonizing habit. Indeed it is not the sermon which is the "exemplum" except insofar as his whole performance is one: the "exemplum" is the Tale. The mock-sermon which began the Prologue has never really been discontinued. Even there, his references to the journey—"Now have I dronke a draughte of corny ale, / . . . my tale I wol bigynne"—seem illusory, distracting, in the more powerful milieu of his preaching. He warned us then that "lewed peple loven tales olde," and we are to hear a series from him, but not yet. "In Flaundres whilom" is a false front. We are back "in this chirche now": but whereas in his Prologue we had a bifocal view of the preacher, while he himself was engaged in shuttling between the real company and his fantasy-congregation in such a way as to weave them loosely together, now there is only a congregation, suddenly and directly exposed to his powers.

> Hir othes been so grete and so dampnable
> That it is grisly for to heere hem swere.
> Oure blissed Lordes body they totere,—
> Hem thoughte that Jewes rente hym noght ynough;
> And ech of hem at otheres synne lough.
> And right anon thanne comen tombesteres
> Fetys and smale, and yonge frutesteres,
> Syngeres with harpes, baudes, wafereres,
> Whiche been the verray develes officeres
> To kyndle and blowe the fyr of lecherye,
> That is annexed unto glotonye.
> The hooly writ take I to my witnesse
> That luxurie is in wyn and dronkenesse.
>   Lo, how that dronken Looth.

Later he differentiates and organizes the vices, but here they are seen tumbling facelessly on one another's heels. We hear many tones, of confidential intimacy, a prurient excitement, pulpit-loud indignation, but all these tones are at play in the one swelling of the voice. The conceit is sharp enough—"Oure blissed Lordes body they totere": its tone *could* be sober, or an indirect attack, or a lament, or it might be a jibe. "Hem thoughte that Jewes rente hym noght ynoghe"; it does begin to sound like a lament, even if the indulgent movement conceals mockery: "And ech of hem at otheres sinne lough." That *could* conclude a lament, but it does not. Rather it breaks up the grouping of possible emotions, as a jester might break up a group on stage. The Pardoner uses the shock, the zest of it, to plunge us with an almost hysterical exultancy (as Speirs describes it) into his "folye": "And right anon thanne comen tombesteres." It is important to be aware of his conversions, just because they are so subtle and rapid. No poetry is more colloquial in the elevated pulpit-manner. But different intonations and implicit forms of involvement are kept latent and volatile in any one sequence. Various ways of feeling the one statement are kept active in the flow of contradictory but mutating emphases. The Pardoner snatches all his effects by surprise, yet with the triumph of logic: a logic hidden in the ambiguous tones and not openly contradicted. Our new relation to him (of congregation to preacher) is proved by a fait accompli: "Lo, how that dronken Looth"—which has the full force of previous smoothly-blending, horribly diverse moral sensations. Later he claims to offer an exemplary dissertation on the deadly sins, but first he enmeshes us in their co-presence, their omnipresence, and in his right to call on Holy Writ now and forever.

He brings a vivacious but breathtakingly calculated play into his relationship with the congregation: a kind of multifaceted play that creates and describes its own audience. We may not notice that he now uses the word "Lordynges" (which in the Prologue pointedly distinguished the company from the "lewed peple") for the congregation in which, here, they are implicitly merged. Even without that, it is thoroughly established that he has only one audience, and that, to take our due part, we must "Looke," "Redeth the Bible," "Looke eek that to the kyng Demetrius." We are (for example) sitting in his pews. But he has no term left in reserve for the superior "company" should he wish to reinstate it.

He makes a fine show of that orthodoxy with which the Sermon is often credited. He uses no privilege not common to late Mediaeval practice "in chirches." His imitations, the "mingling of styles" (to use Auerbach's term), his "realism," are all part of the preacher's licence. So are his cool turnings from one sin to another, and his lists of greater and lesser causes or effects. His strange personality and powers establish themselves in the very play of familiar procedure. But it is not, this Sermon, a thing apart from him, a fine "standard" performance; it has not the independence of the Tale. One feels the play of personality in every clause. His insolence is inseparable from his use of accepted ways of talking.

> Hasard is verray mooder of lesynges,
>
> . . . .
>
> Blaspheme of Crist, manslaughtre, and wast also
> Of catel and of tyme; and forthermo,
> It is repreeve and contrarie of honour
> For to ben holde a commune hasardour.
> And ever the hyer he is of estaat,
> The moore is he yholden desolaat.

"Manslaughtre" and "wast of catel" just bridge the passage between "blaspheme of Crist" and "wast also . . . of tyme," not so that we cannot feel the flick of his contempt, but so that we have no just ground for objecting to it. The whole diminuendo of charges, together with a crescendo of emphases, mock the argument even as its rising exultancy is turned to plaintiveness. Yet he forestalls any objection to his terms (why a "*commune* hasardour"?), using his distinctions ("the hyer . . . of estaat") to renew the smooth flow of his indignation. His final charge, so full of pathos and so daringly a parody of all he has been saying, can neither be assented to (for fear of blasphemy) nor openly reproved.

> Now, *for the love of Crist,* that for us dyde,
> *Lete youre othes,* both grete and smale.

The Pardoner's sermonizing shows a genuine though unstable mixture of impulses: towards the hypocrite's personality-play (as he defined it in the Prologue), and towards the impersonal truth to which his words (in the Tale) have access. It is not astonishing, though, that his "Sermon" should sometimes be taken as an exemplary religious piece, for his remarkable powers are at work in such a way that it is hard to locate their abuses, let alone to discover the whole tendency of his preaching. Our best chance of judging it is against the standard set by the Parson. As *performers* these two cannot be compared: one is incomparable, the other does not perform. But as claimants to the keys of heaven they must be compared, and one realizes that no one can claim those keys within the comic-poetic frame of the journey. The Parson opts out of the frame, and so passes no judgment on any individual, but he does leave a body of impersonal judgments which expose the other preacher. The Pardoner has a hypernatural feeling for the fluidity of sins, of moral impulses, and hence for the deadly possibilities of the least of them; he is a wonderful exponent of the variety and integrity of the inner life. But he can only show it destroying itself: in performance, in its audience. It takes the Parson to show us how directionless are all his exclamations. It is worth setting the unstable flow of impulse in his poetry against the Parson's categorizing prose. The rhythmic repetitions of that are, indeed, not unpoetic:

Seint Paul seith that Sathanas transformeth hym in an aungel of light. / Soothly, the preest that haunteth deedly synne, he may be likned to the aungel of derknesse transformed in the aungel of light. He semeth aungel of light, but for sothe he is aungel of derknesse.

There is a soft, liturgical grandeur in this. One has the sense of a massive harmony waiting in the whole. Each detail exemplifies the wonderfully and rationally connected quality of every part of his moral universe with every other part. Tautology is inexpressibly dignified by his procedures.

> Now comth the synne of hem that sowen and maken discord amonges folk, which is a synne that Crist hateth outrely. And no wonder is; for he deyde for to make concord. / And moore shame do they to Crist, than dide they that hym crucifiede; for God loveth bettre that freendshipe be amonges folk, than he dide his owene body, the which he yaf for unitee. Therfore been they likned to the devel, that evere is aboute to maken discord. /
> Now comth the synne of double tonge. . . .
> Now comth biwreying of conseil. . . .

His analyses penetrate motive, deed and issue often more deeply than do the Pardoner's, though they involve common wisdom at best and cliché at worst. He has no sense of audience. He says "us" and "I seye" completely unselfconsciously, speaking from a constant aware-ness of eternity to the whole community of men. But in the structure of his lists, his relentless continuities, there is a movement continually symbolized and defined by two forces: sin against Christ, suffering by Christ.

> The firste grevance is of wikkede wordes. Thilke suffrede Jhesu Crist withouten grucchyng, ful paciently, whan the Jewes despised and repreved hym ful ofte. / . . . That oother grevance outward is to have damage of thy catel. Theragayns suffred Crist ful paciently, whan he was despoyled of al that he hadde in this lyf, and that nas but his clothes. / The thridde grevance is a man to have harm in his body. That suffred Crist ful paciently in al his passioun. / The fourthe grevance is in outragious labour in werkes. Wherfore I seye that folk that maken hir servantz to travaillen to grevously, or out of tyme, as on haly dayes, soothly they do greet synne. / Heer-agayns suffred Crist ful paciently and taughte us pacience, whan he baar upon his blissed shulder the croys upon which he sholde

suffren despitous deeth. / Heere may men lerne to be
pacient.

There is a continual movement back and forth between his objects.
When he speaks of sins, the prose centres its force on Christ as
suffering them. "Now comth the synne. . . . And no wonder is
. . . / And moore shame do they to Crist." When he speaks of
suffering, strength to endure comes syntactically with the idea of
Christ, "*theragayns* suffred Crist," "*heer-agayns* suffred Crist ful
paciently." And in this constant sense of a human yet perfect
reference-point, particular and symbolic, he finds his forms and
life-force, the steadying energy for his great tract.

The Pardoner has no such reference-point. He does make pathetic
mention of Christ—"Oure blissed Lordes body they totere"—but he
is equally pathetic about "The apostel wepyng . . . / 'I seye it now
wepyng, with pitous voys' "; and indeed he has many objects to
address. He can effect easy divisions of identity (here he becomes the
apostle, and the speaker pitying him, and the sinner he is pitying), and
again and again his hearers are plunged into a limbo of piety, directed
by his eloquence against this or that semi-abstract betrayer.

> O glotonye, on thee wel oughte us pleyne!
>
> . . . .
>
> O wombe! O bely! O stynkyng cod

The passage in which these cries occur contains some magnificently
sensuous and witty analyses of human contradiction, but whenever
he opposes anything to the process of dissolution it is only the
manifestly vacant and voluptuous "O . . . allas . . . O . . . foul."
With these fluid laments and accusations against some
quasi-allegorical enemy, he relieves us of more unpleasantly intimate
charges "Thise cookes," "O dronke man," and brings his hearers
(under him) into a temporary community of conscious innocence.
As part of his dramatic purpose it is superb. But as preaching, his
most lambent discourses show an element of parade and false feeling
that one may miss unless one turns for a standard to the other
sermon, so chaste in its outrage as to be virtually without personal
indignation at all. For the Pardoner passes without pause from
sentimental vacancy to satiric magnificence and back to vacancy in
such a way that we may notice only what is individually brilliant,
and miss its lack of support by any "orthodoxy" of feeling.

Allas! the shorte throte, the tendre mouth,
Maketh that est and west and north and south,
In erthe, in eir, in water, men to swynke
To gete a glotoun deyntee mete and drynke!
Of this matiere, o Paul, wel kanstow trete:
"Mete unto wombe, and wombe eek unto mete,
Shal God destroyen bothe," as Paulus seith.
Allas! a foul thyng is it, by my feith,
To seye this word, and fouler is the dede,
Whan man so drynketh of the white and rede
That of his throte he maketh his pryvee,
Thugh thilke cursed superfluitee.
    The apostel wepyng seith ful pitously,
"Ther walken manye of whiche yow toold have I—
I seye it now wepyng, with pitous voys—
That they been enemys of Cristes croys,
Of whiche the ende is deeth, wombe is hir god!"
O wombe! O bely! O stynkyng cod,
Fulfilled of dong and of corrupcioun!
At either ende of thee foul is the soun.
How greet labour and cost is thee to fynde!
Thise cookes, how they stampe, and streyne, and grynde,
And turnen substaunce into accident,
To fulfille al thy likerous talent!
Out of the harde bones knokke they
The mary, for they caste noght awey
That may go thugh the golet softe and swoote.

It is wildly vivacious, and there are two short passages of the greatest poetry. The first four lines have a sensuousness that is equivalent in Chaucer's clearer diction to much of Shakespeare's. So perhaps, in their thicker, more developed way, do the last lines. They share with the whole passage a yielding quality, certain tones of regret or voluptuous abandonment, and a highly developed sense of life as a self-consuming bodily process in which one existence passes through others in a kind of parody of the Mystical Body. The intervening laments, "I seye it now wepyng," represent (or invoke) a supernatural influence that is impotent or even dead. Perhaps there is a concealed blasphemy, or even a subdued conceit carried on from "substaunce," in the "mary"; at any rate the lines' sensuousness is inseparable from their highly metaphysical judgment. But once passed, the judgment leaves a void. The passage continues into flatness and is followed by one of melodrama. The Pardoner's highest powers are soon dissipated or made over.

His exultant listing of "folye" is mere vicious pleasure at the mingling of ill-practices past the point of analysis or return. His melting sorrow, "O glotonye," accords with his satisfaction at the way distinctions can be lost in a melodramatic imitation of experiential flow. While his sermon-practice is categorizing sins, his sensibility is linking them together, blending antagonistic tones and contradictory feelings, undermining indignation as well as belief. There can be no really purposeful movement while this happens; too many forces are busy neutralizing each other. Qualities of exalted regret, hypocritical accusation, and contempt flow into one another, and again contrast, sharply, even sickeningly. And this sensation of slight sickness, almost of vertigo, accompanies us throughout the Pardoner's witty and exact re-creation of his preaching as in a church. The sensation is produced, if I am right, by a mingling of the immiscible: the Pardoner's will and his capacity; his personality and his "law."

His Tale replaces him almost instantaneously, and he reappears, at the end, only to maintain its decorum as "som moral thyng" by forestalling just that prurient excitement (here over the death-throes) which betrayed the Tale's false beginning. Almost at a signal, "What nedeth it to sermone of it moore?" his sermon-practice springs into full play again, buffeting the air, each sin detached (somewhat on the lines of "Is this a dagger that I see before me?"), held up to view, bravely confronted by the Pardoner and accused. Only now he suddenly compounds everything:

> O *cursed synne* of alle cursednesse!
> O traytours homycide, O wikkednesse!
> O glotonye, luxurie, and hasardrye!
>
> . . . .
>
> *Allas! mankynde,* how may it bitide
>
> . . . .
>
> Thou art so fals and so unkynde, allas?
>   *Now goode men,* God foryeve yow youre trespas.

He is at the height of his assertions of power—"Into the blisse of hevene shul ye gon"—and all he needs to complete the fantasy built into the whole sermon–drama is (as his hypnotic emphases suggest) that the "peple's" "wolle" should assent to his. As he swoops back to acknowledge the company as such, he catches up their physical situation into his symbolic church-setting: "kneleth heere adoun." He offers the pilgrimage an image of itself, a gloriously impudent parody of a Christendom ever journeying towards heaven, ever renewing itself in all its parts.

> Or elles taketh pardoun as ye wende,
> Al newe and fressh at every miles ende,
> So that ye offren, alwey newe and newe,
> Nobles or pens, whiche that be goode and trewe.

The caress ("al newe and fressh") livens the evocation of an ordered society and the sensation of an actual progress. The point is that we *can* visualize it. The comic-apocalyptic threat—"Paraventure ther may fallen oon or two / Doun of his hors, and breke his nekke atwo"—completes his new version of what they are doing. It lays claim to an almost excessive realism, even while it carelessly takes up, *uses* their journey and their persons as figures of fantasy. It is a little like the threat made to Alice, "Why, you're only a sort of thing in his dream!" It is as if the pilgrims were invited to prove their existence, their free "wolle," by doing as he asks. Not only has he left his drama unfinished and "requiring," but each item has a certain claim on them.

> I rede that oure Hoost heere shal bigynne,
> For he is moost envoluped in synne.

In the frame of the prologues it is absolutely true. The Host is "moost envoluped" in humanity. He must answer for them.

So he does, and, far from going out "bang!—just like a candle!" he asserts a grand comic *non serviam* by which the pilgrimage is more firmly established than ever. If there was comic passion in his *wordes . . . to the Phisicien,* there is comic sobriety here. There he used a comic norm to protect himself (and everyone) from the divine standard. Now it is used to protect them from the worst corruption of it. " 'Nay, nay!' quod he, 'thanne have I Cristes curs!' " His "hogges toord" is the price he puts on the "pigges bones." The Pardoner's *reductio* to silence is the most emphatic of any. The narrative holds him up to a disdainful view ("This Pardoner") and confirms "oure Hoost":

> "Now," quod oure Hoost, "I wol no lenger pleye
> With thee, ne with noon oother angry man."

That is a judgment on the whole "jape" inspired by a rage against the "game." The words restore our sense of present time, and the Knight intervenes to check any anarchic tendency by restoring past and future to this "Now":

> But right anon the worthy Knyght bigan,
> Whan that he saugh that al the peple lough,
> "Namoore of this, for it is right ynough!"

The Piers Plowman atmosphere revives, with its stir, its communal "bisynesse," but it is modified by a feudal authority exercised on only this occasion. "Right anon" is the Knight's prerogative here, not the people's, and his "bigan" is more considered than their "gonne to crye." It is his privilege to reaffirm for "al the peple" continuity and an aspiration for the future.

> "I prey yow that ye kisse the Pardoner.
> And Pardoner, I prey thee, drawe thee neer,
> And, *as we diden, lat us* laughe and pleye."

The narrator effects it at once, and then mellows the preterite-glow around this kiss of peace by renewing the present tense: "Anon they kiste, and ryden forth hir weye." The symbolic event is left behind. The riding on perpetuates their common existence, which can neither realize nor abandon its aspirations in the prologue-scheme of a history, but which has a new glow and a deeper resonance after the Pardoner-event.

The final dimension of time is invoked only by the Parson's Sermon and the author's Epilogue. The Pardoner attempted to destroy all sense of time with his invocations. To his threat of doom ("Paraventure ther may fallen oon or two"), the Host replies with another which, in a light and qualified form, foreshadows the Parson's "shal be" of Heaven and Hell: "Lat be . . . / They *shul be* shryned in." The Knight's more discreet, or more timid, "I prey yow" and "lat us" attempt to suspend time a little so that an aspiration may be formulated. The Parson's Sermon supersedes time, in an inexorable sequence of universal laws and exhortations and in another glimpse altogether of the future. It is not "wol," nor the "lat us" of common aspiration, but a promise from outside the scheme: it finds a certain resonance within the light comic-apocalyptic threats, but there is no formal preparation for the Parson's tone when he directs us to heaven in a rhythm which sums up his theology:

> Thanne shal men understonde what is the fruyt of pen-aunce; and, after the word of Jhesu Crist, it is the endelees blisse of hevene, / . . . ther as is . . . ther as is . . . ther as ne is. . . . / This blisful regne may men purchace by poverte espiritueel, and the glorie by lowenesse, the plentee of joye by hunger and thurst, and the reste by travaille, and the lyf by deeth and mortificacion of synne.

The poet follows him with the only simple "confessioun" in the *Tales;* and he does not make it as a pilgrim, only as author:

> so that I may been oon of hem at the day of doom that shulle be saved.

This is a general future state outside the poem's scope: "shal," "is," "may," "shulle be." It leads us to the threshold of an unknown Christendom: the region of "Revelacioun" which it does not seek to enter.

The "Floating" Fragment

Donald R. Howard

The Pardoner's sermon is in a manuscript fragment (Fragment 6) which seems to have no place at all among the others. It contains the Physician's and Pardoner's tales. They belong to no group, have no link with another tale, contain no reference to time or place. The "alestake" mentioned in line 321 might be anywhere: it is a place abstracted from topography, probably a symbol. Nor do the manuscripts give the fragment any consistent place in the order of tales. Thematic considerations are no help: the Physician's Tale might be part of the marriage group; and since lawyers and physicians were rivals it may be significant that it is a pious story like the Man of Law's Tale. But these are not impressive reasons for placing it after the marriage group or after the Man of Law's Tale. Why Chaucer linked the Physician's and Pardoner's tales is a further difficulty; no relationship asserts itself as one does, for instance, between Miller and Reeve or Clerk and Merchant. The two tales come together but stand apart from the rest.

The Physician's Tale reflects his mentality. If it is one of the ideal narratives (it is not, like the others, in stanzas) it is a dramatic example of misguided moralism: he praises virtue in a tale that is morally revolting. This suits the portrait of him in the General Prologue, which lists generic traits: he loves gold, is in league with apothecaries, has advanced knowledge of astrology, knows old as

---

well as recent medical books. Medicine is not and never was an exact science, but Chaucer informs us that he possessed not only learning but the skill or art of healing:

> He was a verray, parfit practisour:
> The cause yknow, and of his harm the roote,
> Anon he yaf the sicke man his boote.
>
> (ll. 422–24; line numbers conform with
> F. N. Robinson, 2d ed.)

To this he added the proverbial sentiment that his study "was but litel on the Bible." The passage ends with the barbed remark that gold, being a cordial in "physik," was what he especially loved. He is a character still familiar: the perfectly competent physician whose primary interest is money. The most notable detail is his association with pharmacists: "ech of hem made other for to winne— / Hir frendship nas nat newe to biginne."

The Physician's inordinate love of gold suggests something askew in his motives and ideals. It is not just that he is thrifty; it is that he got rich from the Black Death, for which no physician knew a cure—"He kepte that he wan in pestilence" (l. 442). That many doctors did so was among the scandals of the age. His motive is evidently *pure* avarice—he is not in love with buying land like the Man of Law, nor with airs and pretensions like the Franklin, nor with *making* money like the Merchant, but with gold itself, with *having* it. In a credit economy money has a specterlike quality, but avarice in the fourteenth century would have been more primitive; moralists compared it to idolatry. And gold, that most precious metal, was the principal object of avaricious veneration. This might be seen as a possible link between the Physician's and Pardoner's tales, for avarice is the Pardoner's besetting sin and avarice for gold central to his sermon. But the Physician's *tale* has nothing to do with avarice: it is a pious tale about the preservation of virginity, which Chaucer adapted perhaps from Livy as well as the *Roman de la Rose*. It has no headlink or introduction, but the manuscripts consistently attribute it to the Physician. There is no sure suggestion of a date, though it seems unlikely that it would have been written after 1390, for it shows no influence from the version in Gower's *Confessio Amantis;* one can imagine that it was written in earlier times, when Chaucer was sharing materials with Gower, and attributed to the Physician later. Perhaps it shows the Physician as a sententious moralizer and thus (given the slur on his morals in the General Prologue) a hypocrite. If that is true, he falls into a class with other moralizers who do not practice what they preach, among them the Pardoner.

The way he tells his tale, not its subject, is what reveals his mentality. He is full of high-minded advice for parents and governesses (ll. 72–104)—thinks it very important they teach virtue by precept and example. His tale is baldly allegorical: the twelve-year-old virgin is named Virginia, her father Virginius. She is beautiful—Nature, he goes on at length, never created a lovelier. The villain, a false judge named Apius, desires her; with bribes and threats he gets a local churl to appear in court and plead that Virginia is his servant and has been abducted by Virginius. Apius, presiding over this kangaroo court, passes judgment before Virginius has defended himself. Virginius goes home and in operatic fashion addresses Virginia: she has two ways, death or shame, and he ruefully chooses death. She answers "O mercy, deere fader! . . . Is there no grace, is there no remedye?" "No, certes, deere doghter myn," he answers. In her aria that follows she embraces her cruel fate, thanking God she will die a maid. The father then beheads his daughter and brings the head to Apius, who sentences him to hanging. For the finale a thousand people rush in, knowing of the judge's wickedness, and imprison him. He kills himself, and all others "consentant" to the crime are hanged, save only the churl Claudius, who is exiled on Virginius's magnanimous plea. "Here," concludes the Physician, "may men seen how sin hath his merite." What he means is that sinners will be struck down *in this life;* it is all very simple, like revenge tragedy or revenge itself. The moral is, forsake sin or sin will forsake you.

That is like the moral of the Pardoner's Tale, and if the two come back-to-back for any reason it is because of the contrast they afford. In the Pardoner's Tale a grim and secret force which punishes evil springs naturally and with a mysterious rightness from wicked deeds themselves. In the Physician's tale this element of wonder and terror is lacking: his is a coldly rational world in which a father can save his daughter's virtue by killing her, in which sinners get killed off mechanically. Underneath it all is a tacit feeling that life is cheap. And who more than an avaricious physician would be likely to harbor this callous estimate of human life? I have been talking as if the Physician made up the tale, but he begins by announcing that it is from Livy. Like Polonius he is keen on the classical background. The tale follows its stoic source closely, not that this makes it the less harsh. The question whether death was preferable to losing virginity by rape was not a new one; Chaucer would have known St. Augustine's verdict that such deaths, however pious their motives, are not necessary because chastity is of the mind not merely of the body. Chaucer's two additions to his sources (ll. 35–120, 207–53) emphasize the tale's two most characterizing elements. In the first he adds to the description of Virginia's beauty a passage attributing to her a panoply of virtues, this followed by the address to governesses and parents. In the second he adds the father's final address to his daughter and the daughter's reply. The first highlights the sententious quality of the Physician's moralism, the second the single-minded way he sees the solution. Of course life *was* cheap in the Middle Ages, violence and sudden death were a part of everyday existence, and people were sticklers for virginity in unmarried daughters. But other tales present alternatives to the Physician's cold moralism; one cannot imagine the Parson subscribing to his view without making plenty of distinctions. That Chaucer himself could view without skepticism the picture of a father beheading his daughter to preserve her virtue and presenting the head to her tormentor is beyond all possibility. But a physician grown rich from the plague would be less sensitive. The grotesque tale and its grisly morality is a suitable prologue to the Pardoner's "moral tale." Simplistic as his tale is, the Physician must really think he loves virtue; but the Pardoner is not so unsubtle.

The Pardoner with his "compeer" the Summoner is a pariah among the pilgrims, and his tale seems to be in a similar position among the other tales—the fragment it belongs to is sometimes called the "floating" fragment. You can put the fragment in any of the gaps in the existing structure (between Fragments 1 and 2, 2 and 3, 5 and 7, or 7 and 8) and manufacture a literary or thematic relationship, but none asserts itself. I mean to suggest that it belongs in the no-man's land where it is, "floating" on the periphery of the interlaced structure. Doesn't Chaucer suggest this himself by putting the Pardoner last in the General Prologue, like an unpleasant thought nudged out of the narrator's memory as long as possible? The Pardoner's Prologue and Tale get where they belong by a seemingly strange artistic rightness, but this rightness is owing to convention: medieval art had a place for the grotesque, but it was never at the center of things—it was on the outside or the underside. Chaucer lived a century before Bosch and then Breughel isolated this estranged world, nearly a century before the world "grotesque" came to be applied to ancient art discovered in grottos. In his time the grotesque—the disordered, incongruous, and startling element in experience, the *demonic* element—was antithetical to artistic ordering or structuring; its place was at the periphery, but there it was permitted to exist and did exist. There is a right place for the Parson's "sermon" at the end of the work; the Pardoner's anti-sermon, coupled with the Physician's Tale, belongs in no ordered structure.

"Modernizing" Chaucer

Donald R. Howard

The force of [the Pardoner's] envy and self-contempt is supercharged with the energy of aggression. The ritual of pardon-selling becomes a habitual fraud, and this becomes a compulsion; he must get more and more because nothing that he gets can satisfy—nothing can unleash upon others the venom he would like to unleash, nothing provide what is missing in him of potency, renunciation, repentence. Hence the energy of detail and of rhetoric with which he catalogues the objects of his evil will—his substitutionary lusts tumble helter-skelter off his tongue: "I will" (which meant to choose) is repeated over and over:

> What, trowe ye, that whiles I may preche,
> And winne gold and silver for I teche,
> That I wol live in poverte willfully?
> Nay, nay, I thought it never, trewely!
> For I wol preche and beg in sundry landes,
> I wol nat do no labour with myn handes,
> Ne make baskettes, and live thereby,
> By cause I wol nat beggen idelly.
> I wol noon of the apostles countrefete;
> I wol have money, woole, cheese, and whete
>
> . . . .
>
> Nay, I wol drinke licour of the vine,
> And have a jolly wench in every town.
>> (ll. 439–53; line numbers conform
>> with F. N. Robinson, 2d ed.)

From *The Idea of the* Canterbury Tales. © 1976 by the Regents of the University of California. University of California Press, 1976.

So when he turns to the pilgrims he cannot resist a similar catalogue of his greeds:

> Myn holy pardoun may you all warice,
> So that ye offre nobles or sterlinges,
> Or elles silver brooches, spoones, ringes.
> Boweth your heed under this holy bulle!
> Cometh up, ye wives, offreth of youre woole!

In explaining this compulsion, Professor Kellogg has shown how he progresses through that concatenation of vices implicit in the idea of the Seven Deadly Sins—from pride to envy, from envy to wrath, from wrath to despair, after which the sinner can only wallow hopelessly in sins of the flesh, gluttony, avarice, and lechery, hoping to regain through the flesh what he has lost in the spirit.

This progression in his sinning is why the Augustinian pattern is demonstrably present in the presentation of him—why the exegetical tradition with its "scriptural" eunuch is demonstrably present: because Chaucer, like St. Augustine, could look at those men whom a Christian age called sinners and see in them what we now call a neurotic circle, self-feeding, in which every defeat provokes the motive for a new action and every action provokes a new defeat. The Augustinian conception of evil did not last into and beyond Chaucer's time merely because it was Augustinian. It lasted because St. Augustine was a shrewd and articulate observer of human conduct: what he said squared with the realities of human behavior a thousand years after he wrote it and does still. Hence when I talk about neurosis and compulsion the reader must not think I am "modernizing" Chaucer; it is the opposite—I am using the lexicon of our time to name kinds of behavior which the medievals *already knew*. Psychological realism used to be all any critic saw in Chaucer; now critics want to see Chaucer's characters "in Chaucer's terms," which means "sources" and "background" and "convention." The Pardoner becomes a copy of Faux-Semblant and a "scriptural eunuch." But such opinions ignore the nature and the meaning of literary tradition; for a literary tradition is nothing more than a set of conventions by which the artist perceives reality—it *is* the artist's "terms." One can argue that medieval men were all reasonable zombies who held identical opinions and saw everything in moral, not psychological, terms; but to argue this one has to ignore everything they wrote about people's motives, their inner states, their dreams, their moral choices, and their souls.

Behind the conventions and the "background" in the Pardoner's Prologue and Tale lies the actual horror with which the Middle Ages viewed guilt. Guilt was produced by misconduct and was a torment; hence sin was its own punishment, leading to a process which is self-punishing and, at a certain secret point, irreversible. Since guilt is a torment, the sinner wishes to flee that torment; and his only choice, unless he repents, is to flee into further misconduct by wallowing in sins and lusts, all of which produce more guilt. Repentance is always a possibility until at a secret moment the scale is tipped; then it was said God had given them up to the lusts of their own hearts. The moment when the scale tipped was the moment of despair. Pride, envy, and wrath produced despair. The anger which surges under the Pardoner's behavior, this charge of aggressive energy fed by frustration and guilt, must at some point break down. Despair (*acedia*) is the failure of hope, and hope—the expectation of God's mercy—is essential to the Christian life. To give up hope is to call into question the mercy of God, to be unable to repent. And at this point the sinner engages in a turmoil of self-indulgence, envy, and frustration which collapses into a state of listlessness and inactivity. The process is repetitive and cumulative: the sinner does not fall into an irreversible vegetative *acedia*: rather, the *acedia* feeds anew the flames of his wrath, envy, and pride. The only release is from the entrapping chain of cause and effect; and the longer one waits the harder release comes. This self-destroying quality of guilt was, in the thought of the Middle Ages, the ultimate grotesquerie: it was that part of worldly experience which would end in damnation, would be estranged forever.

The Pardoner's Tale as Dream and Happening

How do we know the Pardoner experiences this inner torment? Because he projects it unconsciously into his sermon. The medieval sermon normally used exempla as a means of illustrating a point; the Pardoner, knowing that "lewed" people love old stories, bloats up an exemplum so that it subsumes all else, cleverly keeping up interest while he inveighs against other sins in digressions; this organization helps him keep avarice central. Ostensibly the exemplum shows how the rioters brought death upon their heads because of avarice. And it does show this, probably, to the "lewed" people. But from the reader's point of view it reflects the Pardoner's own inner conflict. The three rioters are a projection of himself. They are sinning in a tavern while Death stalks outside: taking the personification literally they attempt to "slay" Death. Told where Death is, they find not a person but bushels of gold florins, and each plots, Cain-like, to kill his "brothers" in order to have more for himself; thus all "find death."

The events happen in an unaccountable and unmotivated way—characters appear and disappear unpredictably. There are abrupt junctures, as in dream-visions. Many allegorical meanings have been suggested, especially for the old man, but what stands out about him is that he is old (he is depicted with the conventional iconography of Old Age, cloak and staff) and says he desires death. Alfred David convincingly treats him as an archetype. Pinning down such allegorical meanings in the tale involves reading it for content, but the form and tone are what make it so haunting. Its dreamlike quality makes it *sound* like an allegory, but then medieval allegories normally *were* figured as dreams, and it has one quality which makes it far more like a dream than like an allegory: it is an exceedingly personal projection, so much so that everything in it can be related directly to the Pardoner's consciousness. The dream is about three nameless rioters who commit all the same sins as the Pardoner himself; they are "younge folk," and the Pardoner seems to think of himself that way—"teche us younge men of your practike," he has asked the Wife. Upon them, as inwardly upon himself, he showers down a rain of moral disapprobation. It is not only that they are wicked; their wits are dulled, so that they talk in non sequiturs and repeat *idées fixes* as drunks do; and in this they mirror his own obstinacy, the clouding of his intellect which accompanies the progressive weakening of his will. He relates their vices with the same compulsive catalogues he has used to name his own lusts; puts them in a tavern ("the Devil's temple") like himself, and in the Devil's service: they

> haunteden follye
> As riot, hasard, stewes, and tavernes,
> Where as with harpes, lutes, and guiternes
> They daunce and playen at dees bothe day and night,
> And ete also and drink over hir might;
> Thurgh which they doon the devil sacrifise

> Within that devils temple, in cursed wise,
> By superfluitee abhominable.

And they are, like himself, vainly boastful of their sins and eager to encourage sin in others—"ech of hem at otheres sinne lough" (l. 476).

The events of the tale are a series of dreamlike entrances and exits, unprepared and unmotivated. A bell rings and a corpse is carried in. A reveller, undistinguishable from the others, tells a boy to find out who it is. The boy was already told two hours *before:* it was an old companion of theirs, slain suddenly sitting drunk on a bench, by a "privee theef men clepeth Deeth" who (like the boy and the old man) then "went his way withouten wordes mo." Now for the first time (l. 679) we learn that a plague is going on (the plague was sometimes called The Death). At last the boy innocently tells "what his mother told him" and then disappears:

> Me thinketh that it were necessarie
> For to be war of swich an adversarie.
> Beth redy for to meet him everemore—
> Thus taughte me my dame; I say namore.

The rioters now fall into one of those absurd, literal-minded arguments familiar in taverns and in dreams. God's arms! says one, is it so dangerous to meet him? I'll go looking for him. With curses he gathers the others in a drunken huddle for ritual oaths of brotherhood: they will slay Death before nightfall. Now they are off to the village, trailing a babble of grisly oaths whose purport is "Death shall be dead." At the heart of their self-delusion is a trick which language itself plays on them: they misread a figure of speech, taking it literally. Half a mile gone, as they are about to climb over a stile, they meet an "old man and a povre," all wrapped up except his face. The proudest of the revellers asks him why he lives so long: they take his answer no less literally, missing his hints. The old man arrives as suddenly and unpredictably as the young boy; his speeches are as specterlike and pointedly true; and he disappears from the scene as suddenly.

These episodes joined by dreamlike junctures are thematic more than narrative. They single out in abstraction truths which press upon the Pardoner's consciousness; and they are presented with the intensity and visualization characteristic of the dream-vision. To-

gether the boy and the old man suggest youth and age—conceptions
of innocence and experience which exist in the Pardoner's mind, each
with its own character and its own kind of truth. The innocent boy
speaks simple childlike sentences, trails off with simple good sense—
"thus taughte me my dame." The weary old man talks in meander-
ing, circuitous sentences, runs on about his plight: however far he
wanders he can find none who would exchange their youth for his
age, nor will Death take his life, nor will Mother Earth let him in. In
two ways the old man's discourse parallels the young boy's,
expanding upon the suggestions of the child as experience might be
expected to expand upon innocence: (1) As the boy ended with his
mother's lesson, the old man ends with the chilling, plaintive address
to the ground, his "mother's gate," that is, the grave, which like the
womb can offer him peace or let him be born anew. He says he will
give his worldly possessions in return only for a haircloth to be
wrapped in:

> on the ground, which is my modres gate,
> I knocke with my staff, both erly and late,
> And saye "Leeve moder, let me in!
> Lo how I vanish, flesh, and blood, and skin!
> Alas! whan shull my bones been at reste?
> Moder, with you wolde I chaunge my cheste
> That in my chambre longe time hath be,
> Ye, for an heire clout to wrap in me!"
> But yet to me she wol nat do that grace,
> For which full pale and welked is my face.
>
> (ll. 729–38)

This awesome portrayal of a soul cast adrift by its mother into an
unwanted life, toward a death wished for and denied, reflects the
Pardoner's spiritual plight—it expresses his longing for oblivion, for
a return to the womb, or for another birth; and it portrays a
circumstance, like his own, in which no such release is permitted.
(2) As the boy's short discourse is a warning to the rioters, the old
man's garrulous discourse is even more ominous. He twice quotes
Scripture—that one should rise before an old man (Lev. 19:32) and
do him no harm (Ecclus. 8:7). This would sound like the self-
centered, querulous murmurings of the very old, except that it ends
with an eerie reverberation of the Golden Rule—"Namore than that
ye wold men did to you / In age"—to which he pointedly adds "if

that ye so long abide." Blessing them, he concludes "I moot go thider as I have to go," but they hold him back, demanding to know where Death is. His directions are equally ominous—he sends them up a "crooked way" where he left Death under a tree (remarking slyly "Nought for your boost he wol him no thing hide"); the details suggest the Way and the Fall. He blesses them again, then drops from the picture:

> God save you, that bought again mankinde,
> And you amend.

This last word, "amend," is hauntingly double-edged: it may mean "improve," which suggests he knows their evil, or "make amends with," as is to be the case.

The Pardoner is an ironist, and one can be sure that he takes some satisfaction in the hidden warnings of this last scene: it is ironic that the rioters do not get the point. But it is doubly ironic that in real life the Pardoner is no less blinded. In what follows, the "amends" brought down upon the revellers compound the irony. We see significance everywhere of which the personages in the story are unaware; and we watch an outcome take shape which is the reverse of what they expect. The situation itself generates irony, and the Pardoner capitalizes on this. When the rioters run to the tree and find almost eight bushels of gold florins, the Pardoner adds "No lenger thanne after Deeth they soughte." He has one of them say that Fortune has given them the money to live their life "in mirth and jolitee." Then their greed is turned upon each other—the youngest is knifed by the older two, leaving behind him the poisoned bottles from which his slayers drink in celebration. Thus the gold is their death and good Fortune is ill. It is a fabliau situation in which all three tricksters are tricked by language and Fortune, by each other, and by themselves.

But the trickster Pardoner is ironically tricked by his own story. As his whole tale in its aura of dreamlike unreality reflects his inner turmoil, its outcome is a warning of his own future which he cannot heed. The greed of the rioters turns into destructiveness—they become divided among themselves and bring death upon their own heads; in the same way the Pardoner, divided against himself, is heading into spiritual death. This dreamlike quality makes his tale share in an irony about life from which no one is free—that what we need to know about ourselves is potentially knowable and sometimes known by others, but often lies beyond our grasp. In medieval terms, his tale has about it the quality of the *somnium coeleste,* a warning from on high which he does not heed. That was the case of the spiritually impotent: the self-knowledge which they stubbornly avoided was "repressed" but attainable by an act of will. They could speak true and not heed the truth they spoke. The Pardoner's tale injects into the presentation of him its most macabre and ironic effect: it makes the *Totentanz* of his inner life dance before us so that we understand how it is possible for him not to see what we see.

The way the Pardoner ends his tale is consistent with everything we know about him, and there is no way of telling whether his attempted joke or trick at the end is an afterthought; he says he forgot to say it, but this could be part of his act, and it would be consistent whether it was an afterthought or not. Not that consistency is necessary in a literary character: an inconsistent or contradictory action is as "real" as any other. When the Pardoner concludes "And lo, sires, thus I preche," he adds a blessing,

> And Jhesu Christ, that is our soules leche,
> So graunte you his pardoun to receive,
> For that is best: I wol you nat deceive.

A blessing is conventional at the end of a tale, but the phrase he chooses is scarcely formulaic or perfunctory. He has made no effort to deceive the company, so there is nothing outrageous in his saying this unless he has already planned the unsuccessful trick which follows. We do not know whether his utterance is sincere or part of his game; likely it is both. "Full oft in game a sooth I have herd saye," says the Host; we can suppose that even if the blessing is part of an effort to hoodwink the company it is sincere at some level of consciousness. Since the Pardoner is an ironist, it is in character that, having said "I wol you nat deceive," he should proceed to deceive them. What does it matter? If they only laugh, he can shrug it off as a joke. Yet he thinks little enough of them to suppose (perhaps rightly) that some at least would be taken in; and he is impudent, dares to confront and challenge them to be his dupes, either by buying his pardons like fools or joining him in an intimate joke against the fools who buy. It is a perfect piece of bravado, for he can pretty well count on the one or the other response. The final speech is another expression of his "method," his bag of tricks, and not a very big risk.

The hiatus between "I wol you nat deceive" and the "after-thought" seems enormous—enough so to make one critic imagine a pause and a hushed silence, and to make editors put a paragraph there. Yet the hiatus is in us, not in the scene: the Pardoner could speak that second line so hard upon the first as to swallow up "deceive." As before, he confronts them with an ironic, mocking challenge. His motive as before is to draw them into his power; and he can do so either by making dupes of them or by making them laugh with him at his own evil. It is a very witty stroke, a gross and exaggerated self-parody: he informs them that they ought to kneel down and meekly receive his pardons, or receive them as they go, anew at every mile's end, so long as they keep offering money—it's a good thing he is there, he adds, because one or two of them might fall off their horses and break their necks, and they are safe in his fellowship since he can absolve them. He lets the specter of Death hover over them again as in his tale; and then he enlists the Host—because he is the leader of the game, because he loves jokes and entertainment, perhaps also because he understands that things said in game are often meant in earnest. The Pardoner may think he sees in him a kindred spirit. Or it may be a self-destructive act on the Pardoner's part—the Pardoner may sense in the Host the one most likely to puncture his moment of triumph—and the Host's anger might be directed at the Pardoner's impulse to spoil his own success.

The Host's response is far more of a surprise than the Pardoner's "afterthought," and is harder to understand because we haven't the insight into the Host that we have into the Pardoner. It is sometimes thought that a bluff male figure like Harry Bailly would be offended by the feminoid Pardoner; but this opinion does not square with human psychology any more than it squares with the text. The Host first addresses the Pardoner "thou bel ami," which is mildly derisive, but he goes on to ask for some mirth or japes in a relaxed way without further comment. Compare his response to the hardy, philandering Monk, a "manly man" in whom he seems to see a threat of cuckoldry or competition: he taunts him cruelly for thirty lines about his sexual prowess and his vows of chastity. And he is not less roughspoken with other pilgrims—"Straw for your gentilesse" he cries at no less a figure than the Franklin. He is not initially rougher to the Pardoner than to others. Besides, for all his appearance of hardy masculinity, the Host is always complaining about his shrewish wife and worrying about cuckoldry. What we need to know is not why the Host "doesn't like" the Pardoner but why he finds this particular speech offensive. One answer is that he is *not* offended—that his retort is a joke of sorts, raucous and overplayed, done without the Pardoner's deft touch; hence it oversteps a bound by hitting at the Pardoner's most vital point. The Host claims he was only "playing" (l. 958) when he sees his outburst greeted by the Pardoner's angry silence; and perhaps, if the Pardoner had answered with some equally extravagant fling, the Host would have taken it in stride. But the Host's language to the Pardoner is very violent: the kernel of his taunt about the Pardoner's "coillons" is framed on either side by images of excrement, and these primitive or infantile expressions of rage are both associated with relics. When he says

> Thou woldest make me kiss thyn olde breech,
> And swere it were a relic of a saint,
> Though it were with thy fundement depaint!

he is probably making a reference to the famous hair breech which St. Thomas wore, one of the most prized relics of the Canterbury shrine—an object which Erasmus was to find revolting. It is likely that it was thought a particular mortification to venerate this relic; Professor Knapp thinks there might have been an old joke about doing so. The Host appropriately swears by St. Helena, who found the ultimate relic, the true Cross, that he would like to have the Pardoner's coillons in his hand instead of relics or "seintuarie": let them be cut off, he says, and I will help you carry them—they shall be enshrined in a hog's turd. It is too specific to be the stereotyped "shit-on-you" kind of insult; but the degree of its cruelty depends on whether the Host is certain from the Pardoner's appearance that he *is* without testicles. Professor Curry was so convincing about the medical symptoms of anorchism that almost everyone since has taken the Host's words as a calculated insult. Yet part of the realism of the passage lies in the fact that we don't know the Host's intentions any more than we would if we were there. Possibly the Pardoner's extravagance is contagious; possibly the Host is carried away by the ingenuity of his swearing and lets slip out something he has suspected but not allowed himself to think about. That is often what people do when they sense or surmise something best not spoken of. We don't know what the Host *means* to do, only what he says and what powerful feeling is behind it.

What trips this feeling off is equally unclear. I like the explanation offered by Gabriel Josipovici, that the Host wants to play the
game by his own rules: "So long as it is he who makes the jokes he
is only too eager to invoke the game as an excuse; but as soon as the
joke turns on him he forgets all about the game and its rules in his
blind anger at the joker. This is just what happens at the climax of the
Pardoner's Tale: as the Pardoner finishes, Harry Bailly finds that for
the first time the joke is on him, and he does not like it" (*The World
and the Book*). But we do not *know* that the joke is on the Host. The
Pardoner, by asking him to join in a joke on the others, hints that the
Host is *not* taken in. The Host recoils from being the Pardoner's
accomplice, but after his outburst he *says* he was joking—("I wol no
lenger play")—and perhaps he believes it. The earnest feeling
beneath his joking does not for that matter have to be anger.
Intimacy is part of the Pardoner's bag of tricks, and he uses the
intimate tone on the Host—"I rede that our Host here shall biginne,
/ For he is most envoluped in sinne." But his timing is off: his tricks
come too fast, and his hurried commands—"Come forth, sir Host,"
"Offre first anon," "unbokle anon thy purse"—push too hard. The
Host is not the kind of man who likes to take orders. And he must
pick up the tense energy of the Pardoner's hasty speech with its
self-destructive possibilities. If there is something compulsive or
automatic in the Pardoner's last effort to trick somebody or everybody, there is something equally compulsive or automatic in the
Host's abusive reply: it is a surge of competitive energy meant to
dominate the Pardoner, to keep himself in power. It tumbles out in
images of excrement and castration, a possible response whether the
Pardoner were a eunuch or not. The remarkable thing about the
passage, and the thing that makes it so right, is that it *just happens*—
fast and inexplicably. It is a happening, not a story. "Stories have a
point and make dramatic sense; their truth is of secondary importance," Christopher Isherwood observes; "happenings do not seem
to make any sense at all." One can well imagine Chaucer *had*
witnessed a scene like it: almost everyone has.

The aftermath of this happening is reported in only thirteen
lines, but there are scarcely thirteen lines anywhere in Chaucer which
accomplish more. The Pardoner's angry silence, for such a manipulator of language as he, is the ultimate defeat; it makes him seem
mysterious, deflated, and sad. It can be viewed as a kind of
martyrdom, or anti-martyrdom. And his silence may be a single ray

of hope, the end of his noisy flight from the warning voice within. When he demands that the Host unbuckle his purse and the Host responds by wishing he had the Pardoner's "coillons" in his hand, the two men have in effect exchanged malevolent wishes to castrate each other. The Pardoner thinks of the Host's "purse" (the word had its inevitable bawdy sense). This is ironic—the purse with money in it is the Pardoner's, not the Host's, surrogate. It is equally ironic that the Host thinks of the Pardoner's "coillons." So it is doubly ironic that what the Host manages to cut off is the Pardoner's tongue, his flow of speech. His paralysis of tongue reminds one of Pandarus after all was lost, "As still as stone, a word ne coude he saye." For Pandarus and the Pardoner are, in all of Chaucer, the two great proprietors of language, glib persuaders who can make others act upon their wills. And the Pardoner's silence is a loss of will: "So wrooth he was, no word ne *wold* he saye." It isn't that he is "speechless," that like Pandarus he *couldn't* speak, but that he has lost the will to—*wold* is the verb used. The Host's reply, as Kittredge pointed out, compounds the injury by calling attention to his wrath; in doing that it calls attention to his defeat. And worse, "all the peple lough."

Then the Knight makes peace between them. It is a courtly gesture which reflects the aristocrat's preference for smooth surfaces; and because the Knight has the highest rank there is good enough reason why he should be the one to step in as keeper of the peace. It is, too, a charitable gesture: if his coming forward "Whan that he saugh that all the peple lough" implies causality, he must feel compassion for the Pardoner. How symbolical the gesture is, I am not sure: if Chaucer meant it for a figure of Christian charity, he would have had the Parson come forward. Nor is the gesture so charitable that the Knight maintains complete impartiality: he seems to side with the Host. "Namoore of this, for it is right enough" could be understood to suggest just deserts, and he calls the Host "ye" and "sir Host," adding "that been to me so deere," while calling the Pardoner "thee." He asks the Pardoner to "be glad and mirrye of cheere" and asks the Host to come forward and make the gesture of peace; this may be a compliment to the Host's sense of justice, but it does treat the Pardoner as the injured party. What the Knight wants, as he says at the close of his speech, is for them to laugh and play as before—he introduces no abstractions or ideals. The last line, "Anon they kiste, and riden forth hir waye," is really the only line which seems symbolical or figural. The kiss can be the "kiss of peace" symbolizing Christian charity and brotherhood, but it can also be (since it is the Knight's idea) the upper-class way of symbolizing peaceful relations.

It is hard to say that because of this one line the ending lapses into the figural style and presents a symbolical gesture which unites courtly civility and Christian charity, but I feel that this is what happens. The gesture *was* symbolical, and the brevity of the scene gives it a spectral, abstract quality. After the drama of the Pardoner's sermon and the unpredictable happening which follows, the figures now seem to move fleetingly, as at a distance—there is the Pardoner's silence, the Host's sulky response ("I wol no lenger playe"), the Knight's decorous charge, the ambiguous ritual act. It is a conclusion in which nothing is concluded, yet readers of the poem seem to agree that it is right.

This could be because such ambiguous endings, in which tensions are left unresolved, seem right to modern tastes. When Professor Kellogg says that the Pardoner's evil "is absorbed into the pattern of existence, and the universe goes on undisturbed," he could be describing the effect produced by a modern novelist. Students of medieval literature often think if a medieval work appeals to a modern taste the appeal must be mistaken, and so scurry off to find an antiquated taste for it to appeal to. But the "modernity" of a passage such as this is nothing more than its power to appeal to subsequent ages, to outlast changes of taste; it may be the first glimmering of a kind of literary effect for which a taste was to develop later. Such effects, and a taste for such effects, are a part of literary tradition, and Chaucer was the principal founder of English literary tradition. There are other medieval works which do not end with a resolution—*Piers Plowman* would be an example—so we could find medieval precedents. If tradition had taken another turn, we would not be able to grasp the "literary" quality of the present passage or respond to its ambiguity. It would only be a puzzle.

But there is another way of responding to the passage which *is* characteristically medieval and not at all modern, and for which we must therefore imagine or acquire a response. The passage takes a circumstance involving psychological realism and permits it to become figural. Throughout the Pardoner's Prologue and Tale there is a tendency in the direction of allegory: the Pardoner's evil has a stark, primal quality, and the dreamlike character of his tale shares with allegory its disembodied, abstract treatment of character and situation. This tendency is now allowed once more to come to the surface; the Knight's decorous speech and the ritual act of peacemaking make the characters seem distant and abstract, where before they had been close-to-hand and lifelike. Emphasis is thrown upon the symbolical act.

The story itself is complete at line 959 where the Host's speech ends. The ending of the Pardoner's Tale is unique in *The Canterbury Tales* because it is the only ending of a tale not told in the pilgrim's own voice. With the Pardoner's ending, "lo, sires, thus I preche," we are returned to the scene of the pilgrimage; beginning at line 956, "This Pardoner answerde nat a word," the narrator reports what I have called a happening. It seems real enough but cannot be explained psychologically. The effect is to put us at a distance from the Pardoner's character and from the final incident itself. This unique "distancing" suggests that the last line is meant to point us further away from the realism of the tale; the last phrase, "and riden forth hir waye," emphasizes the topos of the Way. In the narrator's voice here we catch no attitude, no tone: we may be hearing the naive objectivity of Chaucer the pilgrim or the ironic detachment of Chaucer the man. The mask and the performer behind it harmonize: "Chaucerian" irony becomes identical with Christian charity. There are only a few places in *The Canterbury Tales* where this Chaucerian moment occurs—where we hear a neutral voice which might as well be Chaucer's own: at the end of the Nun's Priest's Tale where the priest's own voice seems to merge with the author's, perhaps in the last lines of the Miller's Prologue, in the Parson's Prologue, and in the Retraction. But the possibility of this Chaucerian moment is always present. The ironic masquerade which produces the narrator makes us aware of the man himself behind it, makes us intuit his thoughts and feel at one with him. The naive pilgrim-narrator with his puppyish enthusiasm for everybody, good and bad alike, is a funny charade of charity which mistakes St. Augustine's dictum to love the man but hate his evil—the narrator doesn't make the distinction. But we know Chaucer does. In moments like these there is a shock of recognition because we glimpse in the writer we are reading the man we have sensed. They are simple moments when we seem to come back to a reality already known, like the moment of waking from a dream or looking up from a book.

Preaching and Avarice
in the Pardoner's Tale

Warren Ginsberg

Unlike the tales of the Knight and the Clerk, no literary ancestor lies behind the Pardoner's Tale which can help to account for certain elements in Chaucer's creation that continue to puzzle and delight us. The Pardoner himself, it is true, certainly owes something to Faux-Semblant of the *Roman de la Rose,* and the tale he tells has numerous analogues, but the personification of Jean de Meung's poem hardly reflects the complexity of the Preacher of Rouncivale, nor has any exemplum yet discovered aroused the controversy his sermon has. Yet in the absence of a direct source, other medieval documents can offer insight into Chaucer's creation. The Pardoner, after all, does declare himself a preacher, and the subject he preaches about is avarice: both the occupation and the sin were much discussed in the Middle Ages. I shall therefore draw upon medieval treatises on preaching, together with homiletic material on avarice and pertinent exegetical traditions, in order to reexamine the Pardoner and the remarkable tale he tells.

I say reexamine because some work has already been done. Since the Pardoner does preach, his sermon has been analyzed to see whether it follows the suggestions found in contemporary *artes praedicandi.* These works set forth the rationale of medieval homilies, commenting on such matters as how and where the preacher should

From *Mediaevalia* 2 (1976). © 1976 by the Center for Mediaeval and Early Renaissance Studies, State University of New York, Binghamton. Unless noted, translations of Latin sources by author.

divide his sermon; not surprisingly the Pardoner's Tale seems to conform to these dicta. Yet, if the mechanics of sermon-making have been noted, what these manuals and other sources have had to say about the kind of man a preacher should be has not. This is unfortunate, for a glance at any number of works that discuss preaching might have offered an answer to one of the more celebrated cruces of the Pardoner's Tale.

Since Kittredge, critics have wondered why the Pardoner must stop to think of "som honest thyng" to tell the pilgrims; in a recent article, John Halverson has summarized the commentators' bewilderment:

> It is inconceivable that a professional homilist like the Pardoner should need time to recall a moral tale, his stock in trade.

Then, like many critics before him, Halverson offers a "psychological" explanation: "the inference seems inescapable that he is reacting ironically to the implied derogation [of the *gentils'* request for a moral tale]." Appealing as this interpretation may be, I think more than psychological inference may guide us here. In a passage of the *De Doctrina Christiana* which was to have great influence, Augustine advises the orator of God's word to prepare himself in the following manner:

> Ipsa hora iam ut dicat accedens, priusquam exerat proferentem linguam, ad deum leuet animam sitientem, ut ructet quod biberit, uel quod impleuerit, fundat.

> When the hour in which he is to speak approaches, before he begins to preach, he should raise his thirsty soul to God, in order that he may give forth what he shall drink, or pour out what shall fill him.
> (trans. D. W. Robertson, Jr.)

Furthermore, Augustine continues, let the man who would both know and teach learn everything which should be taught, and acquire "a skill in speaking appropriate to an ecclesiastic," but when the time comes for speech itself, the preacher should follow the advice of Matthew:

> Take no thought how or what to speak: for it shall be given you in that hour what to speak. For it is not you that speak, but the Spirit of your Father that speaketh in you.

In the later Middle Ages this advice was not forgotten, though direct illumination by divine wisdom became less frequent; therefore a typical *ars praedicandi* by the thirteenth-century French preacher Astazius, while honoring the precept, nevertheless counsels prelates to prepare their sermons beforehand:

> Advertendum quod sancti doctores qui in Ecclesia prae-cesserunt sine sumpto themate praedicabant nec praedica-tionis materiam ordinabant, quia non indigebant aliquo directivo, cum praedicarent Spiritu Sancto inspirante. Unde praedicabant prout Spiritus Sanctus dabat eis. Sed moderni qui non sunt sancti nec divina scientia illustrati, primo antequam praedicent, praedicantionis materiam or-dinare debent.

> We should note that the holy doctors who have preceded us in the Church used to preach without a prepared text, nor did they arrange the material they preached. For they did not need an ordering method, since they would preach with the Holy Spirit inspiring them. Thus they preached as the Holy Spirit gave them. But today, preachers who are not saints nor illuminated by divine knowledge should, before they preach, first arrange the material of their sermon.

The passage in Chaucer now becomes clear. When he grants the pilgrims' request, the Pardoner's words seem almost a direct parody of Augustine's formula:

> "I graunte, ywis," quod he, "but I moot thynke
> Upon som honest thyng while that I drynke."
> (C. 327–28; F. N. Robinson, 2d ed.)

Corny ale is the Pardoner's draught, not spiritual illumination, and when he later describes how he spits out his venom "under hewe / Of hoolynesse, to semen hooly and trewe" (C. 421–22), the Pardoner literally pours out, in the manner Augustine has described, the poison that fills him. Some have seen the cake and ale which the Pardoner consumes as an ironic reference to the Eucharist. This interpretation gains added force when we recognize that the Pardoner is mocking the very act of preaching itself. His inspiration is not the Holy Ghost's, but is his own, and inevitably it will fail.

Even before he speaks, Chaucer has alerted us that the Pardoner's spiritual insight is suspect; yet as dispensator of sound doctrine, the Christian preacher should, indeed must, be alive to the spiritual sense of Scripture. If he is not, if he is a man of the letter and desires worldly wealth rather than his spiritual treasure in heaven, he is then one who adulterates God's word, and he will fall into temptation and the devil's snare. This verse from the First Epistle to Timothy ("But those who desire to become rich, fall into temptation, and into the snare of the devil") was interpreted by Nicholas of Lyra, among others, as referring specifically to preachers. And this verse is especially significant for the Pardoner, as it immediately precedes the sentence he has taken for his theme, *Radix malorum est cupiditas.*

Indeed, the very text in which this sentence appears, Paul's First Epistle to Timothy, was regarded in the Middle Ages as a biblical directive which authorized the use of allegorical interpretation. As a group, the Epistles of Paul to Timothy and Titus came to be known as the *epistolae pastorales,* for, as A. Médèbielle explains, "Elles tracent les règles à suivre pour diriger et instruire le peuple fidèle et pour le choix des ministres sacrés." In this regard the Letters were especially important for Augustine and subsequent preachers in that they taught the disciples what and how they should teach others. Any man, Augustine writes, who teaches in Church should have these three Epistles before his eyes. The substance of what the pastor should teach may be summarized as sound doctrine; to determine what that doctrine was, however, the preacher had to discern the hidden meaning of the text. The whole of the *De Doctrina Christiana,* as well as many other texts, had just this purpose: to teach preachers how to discover the spiritual sense.

Now the Pardoner himself "was in chirche a noble ecclesiaste," (A. 708), and therefore should know how to read a text spiritually; furthermore, the allegorical exposition of the particular scriptural passage of the day was always a common feature in medieval sermons, one which a preacher of the Pardoner's experience certainly would have known and used. Yet because he is a self-confessed, unrepentant sinner, the Pardoner is incapable of admitting anything more than the literal sense of what he says. Thus when he introduces figures such as a dove or an Old Man, figures that seem to call for an allegorical interpretation, we find his dove has nothing to do with the Holy Spirit, but rather is a barnyard purveyor, and the Old Man's too solid flesh blurs whatever symbolic significance he seems to demand. The Pardoner is not a spiritual man, and the very manner of the fiction he tells reveals his lack of faith. In the words of Rabanus Maurus, following Paul, *Symbolum fidei et spei nostrae non scribitur in charta et atramento, sed in tabulis cordis carnalibus.* [The symbol of our faith and hope is not written on paper with ink, but on the fleshly tablets of the heart.] His ghostly heart empty, the Pardoner wears his corporeal heart on his sleeve; an act of audacity and defiance, but ultimately the act of an inwardly hollow man.

That a man as unconcerned with the evils of gluttony and "dronkenesse" as the Pardoner is should eat and drink before he inveighs against these vices seems quite in character. Yet we remember Augustine's exhortation that the preacher give forth what he shall drink. The Pardoner drinks ale, and we may be certain that no thought of that spiritual wine that was a common symbol for divine preaching ever crossed his mind. "*Vinum dicitur divina praedicatio,*" says Alain de Lille; but those who preach "with an eye to human favor or worldly gain" are frauds: they are like the hucksters and innkeepers who Isaiah says "mix wine with water":

> Unde Isaias (1:22): Caupones vestri miscent vinum aqua.
> Ille doctor vel praedicator miscet vinum aqua qui docet vel praedicat intuitu favoris humani vel terreni emolimenti.

Preachers of this sort are especially insidious, for, as Alain notes in his *Summa de Arte Praedicantium,* the "silly and scurrilous words they use have the effect of making their audience somewhat effeminate":

> In illa praedicatione est aqua vino mista in qua puerilia et scurrilia verba, et animos quodammodo effeminantia ponuntur.

Thus with the Pardoner the spiritual draught that fills the good preacher's vessel has not been diluted but actually transformed into the moist and corny ale he guzzles by the wayside; furthermore, those who partake with him are in danger of becoming like him. If his sermon has had the effect the Pardoner intended, he will have made each listener his "ape" (A. 706): not only will the avaricious preacher have fired the pilgrims' desire for his money-increasing relics, but the Pardoner will also have had each buyer mimic him in all his effeminacy. There could hardly be an insult more stinging to the Host, the first customer approached, than to be compared to the effeminate Pardoner. Our innkeeper will have none of it; he reacts violently, and by revealing the Pardoner's wanting virility, he appropriately exposes a symbol of this preacher's spiritual sterility as well.

When the Pardoner compares himself to a dove, the creature he has in mind is similarly of this world, not the next. For when he preaches, the Pardoner takes pains

> to strecche forth the nekke,
> And est and west upon the peple I bekke,
> As dooth a dowve sittynge on a berne.
>
> (C. 395–97)

This image is so effective precisely because it is vividly literal, because it steadfastly refuses to be symbolic. The dove was so common an emblem for the Holy Ghost (and indirectly the spirit that informs the good preacher) in the Middle Ages, one might have seen even "lewed" folks' eyebrows rise when the Pardoner appropriates it for himself. Yet the man is consistent: spiritual understanding is absent, the tangible reality is all.

Both the ale the Pardoner drinks and the dove he compared himself to tell us something about the kind of man the Pardoner is. So too, I think, does the oak tree of his *Tale,* under which the rioters find their just reward. This oak seems to have been Chaucer's invention; at least it exists in none of the printed analogues, where one searches in vain for mention of any tree, much less an oak. Usually the treasure is found in a forest or grove, in a cave or river. The oak certainly locates the scene more specifically, yet the tree's allegorical significance also seems a telling comment on the Pardoner and rioters alike.

The Old Man advises the rioters that, if they "be so leef / To fynde Deeth," they should

> turne up this croked wey,
> For in that grove I lafte hym, by my fey,
> Under a tree, and there he wole abyde;
> Noght for youre boost he wole him no thyng hyde.
> Se ye that ook? Right there ye shal hym fynde.
>
> (C. 760–65)

As Death is given an increasingly specific location, from grove, to tree, to oak, to the gold the sinners will soon discover, the Old Man at the same time scores the rioters' increasingly dogged determination to find that "privee theef." The tension thus created is enough to guarantee the scene's success, yet the scene is heightened if the oak symbolizes *duritia desperationis,* the obduracy of despair, as it does in an exegetical tradition, or if we associate it with the idea of hardness and determination, as Chaucer does elsewhere in his work; we sense that the very landscape reflects the inner condition of these men. That avarice, as the root of all evil, was sometimes pictured as the trunk of the tree of the seven deadly sins strengthens our conviction that this oak is not so much a locational marker as it is a signpost. But the rioters do not perceive that the setting in which they find the gold constitutes a warning: to them, the tree is nothing more than a tree. In this they resemble the Pardoner, who also is unaware of any symbolic meaning; they neither see nor understand as they should, nor is this surprising, for their spiritual blindness, as I shall now show, is the result of avarice.

If medieval discussions of preachers and their sermons provide insights into the Pardoner and his Tale, what the commentators had to say about the sin of avarice also ought to prove illustrative. After all, the Pardoner declares himself a covetous man, and the only theme he preaches constitutes the chief condemnation of the vice in Scripture. Avarice was attacked in many tracts and exempla written during the Middle Ages; among these one in particular immediately relates to the Pardoner's spiritual vacuity. In his *Summa de Exemplis,* John of San Giminiano compared the covetous man to a shadow for seven reasons: the third had to do with that shadow which led to inner barrenness:

> Tertio quorum umbra sterilitatis inductiva, quia nihil quasi crescit ubi est continua umbra. Sic semina divinorum verborum non possunt crescere et fructus producere ubi est avaricia et divitiarum cura sollicita.

> The third is the shadow that induces sterility, since almost nothing grows where there is continuous shade. Thus the seeds of divine words cannot grow and produce fruit where there is avarice and anxiety-ridden studying after riches.

Avarice, then, can well be the ultimate cause of the Pardoner's subservience to the letter. It is an especially pernicious sin for a preacher to be guilty of, since it is "the ax of preaching," as

Guilelmus Peraldus puts it in his *Summa de virtutibus et vitiis,* that must eradicate this sin:

> Ad avariciam quasi ad radicem omnium malorum praecipue adhibenda esset securis praedicationis. Frustra laboratur in extirpatione malorum si rami amputantur et radix ista relinquitur.

> The ax of preaching must be applied to avarice especially as though to the root of all evil. He labors in vain to uproot evil if the branches are cut and this root remains.

What exactly was this sin, and what were its effects? The questions are important, for their answers will affect our evaluation of the Pardoner's Tale.

One might begin with the implications of the text the Pardoner knows by heart: "*Radix malorum est cupiditas.*" *Cupiditas,* as the *Glossa Ordinaria* and many other sources tell us, translates the Greek *philargyria,* which strictly means the love of money; not surprisingly, some commentators, including Augustine, read the verse as *radix omnium malorum avaritia.* From this narrow definition avarice quickly grew to have the meaning of any immoderate desire for more than is necessary, be it money or "external goods." Thus avarice was the specific sin of *pecuniae amor,* as it appears in lists of the seven deadly sins, and the sin of excessive avidity for things in general. Using this distinction, the Church fathers were able to reconcile the statement in Timothy with Ecclesiasticus 10:15: The beginning of all sin is pride. Every sin was understood to involve a twofold action: the soul turned away from God in pride, and towards a created thing through avarice. Pride and avarice thus became inseparably linked: whenever the chapter in Timothy was mentioned, a discussion of its relation to the verse from Ecclesiasticus was sure to follow. Some critics have thought the Pardoner overweeningly proud; it would be remarkable were he not so.

As one might expect, avarice was accounted a very grave sin; John of San Giminiano notes how it leads to "spiritual death":

> Similiter, avaricia veneno cupiditatis extinguit vitalem calorem charitatis, et ita est causa mortis spiritualis.

> Similarly, avarice extinguishes the vital warmth of charity

with the venom of cupidity, and thus is the cause of spiritual death.

We remember the Pardoner's telling threat:

> Thus spitte I out my venym under hewe
> Of hoolynesse, to semen hooly and true.
> (C. 421–22)

and realize that the certain victim of the Pardoner's poison is the Pardoner himself.

Peraldus also thought avarice as bad an infirmity of the spirit as there could be:

> inter infirmitates spirituales ipsa est pessima, vel una de peioribus.

> Among spiritual infirmities this [i.e., avarice] is the worst, or one of the worst.

Part of the illness, Peraldus continues, is that the avaricious man refuses to be cured: he holds Christ, the *celestis medicus,* as though he were danger itself: he judges "*tantus medicus quasi ad mortem.*" At the climax of his Tale, the Pardoner prays that Christ, "oure soules leche," grant the pilgrims His pardon, "For that is best, I wol yow nat deceyve" (C. 916–18): the statement is utterly true, and the irony arising from its inapplicability to the Pardoner almost unendurable.

To St. Paul, however, the most pernicious effect of avarice was that, as the root of all evil, it drew men from the faith (1 Tim. 6:10). When the commentators elaborated on this verse, they isolated one further consequence: cupidity leads men into vain and empty speech. Hugh of St. Cher's comment is typical:

> A quibus [faith and good conscience] aberrantes, conversi sunt in vaniloquium.

> Wandering from which, they deal in empty speech.

Bromyard agrees, and in a sermon on the circumcision of the spirit, Bonaventure quotes St. Bernard on 1 Timothy 6:10:

> Habentes victum et vestitum, his contenti simus, spiritualis etiam circumcisio debet esse in omnibus sensibus corporis nostri, videndo, audiendo, gustando, tangendo, paucitate utamur, et maxime in loquendo. . . . Loquacitas

est vitium pessimum, et Deo et hominibus odiosum et displicibile: unde debemus esse circumcisi lingua, id est pauca et utilia loqui.

We have food and clothing: let us be content with these, for one ought to be spiritually circumcised in all our bodily senses. In seeing, hearing, tasting, touching, let us be sparing, and especially in speaking. Loquacity is a most miserable vice, hateful and displeasing to both God and man. Therefore we ought to be circumcised in speech, that is, speaking little and to the point.

Critics have wondered for many years why the Pardoner, his magnificent Tale brought to its moving conclusion, presses on, indulging in what Kittredge called "a wild orgy of reckless jesting." Chaucer, I think, would have replied, "But it is his nature to talk too much"; the Pardoner is an avaricious man, and his many words confess the fact more than he knows.

The Pardoner is literal, and he is literal because he is avaricious. Not only his story, but the very manner in which he tells it, points to his spiritual condition. The subject of the Pardoner's exemplum is, of course, avarice; as we shall now see, the most arresting figure in that Tale, the Old Man, is, with the Pardoner himself, Chaucer's greatest embodiment of the effects of that sin.

The Old Man in the Pardoner's Tale has become something of a *cause célèbre;* so famous, in fact, that he has not only been the subject of articles, but articles on these articles have appeared. The Old Man has been many things to many people: a symbol of Death, Death's Messenger, the Wandering Jew to some, to others Paul's *Vetus Homo,* Old Age, Odin, or literally just an old man. What has caused this embarrassment of interpretation? One reason, it seems to me, lies in the fact that Pardoner presents this figure in exactly the same manner each of his other figures has been presented. Everything about the man seems to cry out for an allegorical interpretation; as a man who lives and dies by the letter, however, the Pardoner has refused to allow him anything but a literal sense. For the reader, the effect is astonishing: we are given no answer; we are left to see for ourselves. We may follow the Old Man's directions blindly, as the rioters do, or we may come to see through their experience that his "wey" is "croked" as Dante's *via* is *diritta.* Yet in any attempt to fathom the meaning of this mysterious guide, there are two considerations at least which I think should guide us. One is that as the man's "greet age" is stressed, we should not be surprised to find him exhibiting some signs of senectitude. The other and more important is that since he appears in what is essentially a sermon on avarice, we might therefore reasonably expect him either to represent the sin or warn us against it. The Old Man does both: in appearance and speech, this figure embodies the vice he speaks against. The Old Man is not Avarice, just as he is not Old Age or any other single state or thing, but it seems he is a man who has suffered the pains of avarice and has since repented. As such he is a walking text on the evils of avarice; understanding him, however, seems to be the reader's prerogative.

What do we know of the Old Man? He appears to be Chaucer's invention, this figure, completely wrapped, save his face, who is asked to justify his existence. "Why lyvestow so longe in so greet age?" the proudest of the three seekers after death demands. The Old Man's answer is his history:

> "For I ne kan nat fynde
> A man, though that I walked into Ynde,
> Neither in citee ne in no village,
> That wolde chaunge his youthe for myn age;
> And therfore moot I han myn age stille,
> As longe tyme as it is Goddes wille.
> Ne Deeth, allas! ne wol nat han my lyf
> Thus walke I, lyk a restelees kaityf,
> And on the ground, which is my moodres gate,
> I knokke with my staf, bothe erly and late,
> And seye, 'Leeve modder, leet me in!
> Lo how I vanysshe, flesshe, and blood, and skyn!
> Allas, whan shul my bones been at reste?
> Mooder, with yow wolde I chaunge my cheste
> That in my chambre longe tyme hath be,
> Ye, for an heyre clowt to wrappe in me!'
> But yet to me she wol nat do that grace,
> For which ful pale and welked is my face."
>
> (C. 721–38)

Let us begin with the chest. Robinson assures us that this is a clothes chest, not a coffin; recently, however, commentators have suggested that it might be a money chest, "filled with the florins that he has been hoarding." This I think an exceedingly tempting interpretation, for it provides a strong structural link between the Old Man and the gold (he has left it by the oak, rather than has discovered it there), and it lends, as we shall see, great power and meaning to his words. Unfortunately, evidence to support this claim has been, for the most part, conjecture; some will ask, with Alfred David, "Where is this chamber with the chest full of possessions that he says he would exchange for a hair-cloth?" Once again, medieval sermon books suggest an answer.

Among the many exempla that illustrated the addicting power of avarice, one seems to have particularly appealed to preachers. The version given here is the liveliest, and was reported by Owst in his *Literature and Pulpit in Medieval England:*

> When a certain very rich rustic, who was hard-hearted both to the poor and towards his own soul, had amassed so much wealth that he had a chest filled with money and other treasures, he had it set in front of him as he lay sickening on his deathbed. By the time that the priest could be summoned to make his Will, the sick man had already lost power of speech. The priest, accordingly, suggested a plan to his wife and brother, whereby a "Ha!" from the patient might be taken to indicate approval of what was proposed to him, and silence as the mark of disapproval. Having won agreement for his plan, our priest said to the testator—Do you wish to bequeath your soul to God after your decease, and your body to Mother Church for burial?, and the latter replied, "Ha!" Then the priest said to him—Do you wish to leave twenty shillings to the fabric of your church, where you have chosen to be buried? But the other made no reply and kept a complete silence. Forthwith the priest pulled him violently by the ear, whereat the man cried—"Ha!" Then the priest said— Write down twenty shillings for the church fabric: for see, he has granted it with his "ha!" After that the priest pondered how he could get for himself the chest with the aforesaid treasure. So he said to the sick man—I have some books, but I have no chest to keep them in. That coffer over there would be most useful to me. Would you like me, therefore, to have that coffer to put my books in? But

the other said nothing whatever to these remarks. Then the priest pinched his ear so hard that those who were present declared afterwards that the pinch drew blood from the man's ear. Then the enfeebled rustic, in a loud voice, said to the priest before them all—O you greedy priest, by Christ's death, never shall you have from me as much as a farthing of the money which is in that chest! Having spoken thus, he turned to his devotions and expired. Accordingly, his wife and relatives divided the money between them. This happened in England, so it is said.

Bromyard tells a similar story of a dying man who had lost his power to speak. The priests who were standing about him saw he was near death, and urged him to think of his soul. They shouted in his ears that if he wished to receive the sacraments, he should at least make some sign with his hands, mouth, or face, but they were unable to get any sign from him. Then a certain associate of the fellow said:

> ego cito habebo ab eo signum et apposuit manum ad cistam que erat ad pedes eius in qua erat pecunia sua et cor suum et thesaurus suus quasi volens eam aperire vel apportare et statim quasi expergefactus et quasi nitens caput erigere et voce et vultu triste signum vite ostendit.

> I will quickly get a sign from him, and he placed his hand on the chest which was by his feet, as though he wished to open it or carry it away. In this chest was the fellow's money and his heart and his treasure, and immediately, as if startled from sleep and striving to raise his head, he speedily gives a sign with sad face and voice.

In another story, Bromyard speaks of a man who, when he was to be given extreme unction, hid his right hand from sight. The priest asked him where his hand was and why he did not bring it forth, and the man replied, "*Sub me teneo in ea clavem ciste mee.*"

This is the kind of chest, then, that the Old Man offers to change for a "heyre clowt"; before all else, we should realize the magnitude of the transaction. A "clowt" is a piece of cloth, next to nothing; indeed, the words began to acquire this figurative meaning in Middle English, a userer "wold not gyff þerfor þe valour of a sh[red] clowte." Yet the Old Man would willingly exchange his chest for it. If the chest were filled with treasure, he would indeed be giving up all that he had. Unlike the dying men in the exempla, it seems our venerable figure has renounced the sin of avarice; by wishing to clothe himself in a hair-shirt, a traditional emblem for penance, he indicates that he would like to do satisfaction for his sin. The Old Man's affinities with the Wandering Jew would indicate that, in Dewey Faulkner's phrase, "like the Jew, he is being forced to wander eternally for having offended God grievously in some way." Avarice, I submit, has been the offense, and the Old Man's wandering, his penance.

But why does the Old Man offer to exchange his chest with his mother, the earth? John Steadman has noted that commentators writing against cupidity would frequently portray the earth as the mother a man must return to stripped of his worldly possessions. Due to the nature of the sin, the earth often chides the avaricious man: "Hear," cries Alain de Lille against the miserly man, "hear what the elements declare against you, and especially the earth, your mother. Why dost thou do injury to your mother, why bearing violence against me, who produced you from my bowels?" Chaucer reverses the situation: the Old Man pleads with the earth, and the sincerity of his petition makes us feel that his repentance has been long-standing and heartfelt.

If we look at the Old Man in this way, as a repentant sinner, we can also see why he is old. Chaucer might have gotten the idea from the sixth chapter of the Epistle to Timothy, the same chapter that gave him the Pardoner's theme. The Old Man quotes Paul's precepts to the rioters, though without much effect. Innocent III's *De Contemptu Mundi* might also have contributed to the character's formation. At least since Seneca, however, avarice has been the bane of the old: *Caeteris vitiis in homine senescentibus, sola avaritia juvenescit* [When the other vices in man have grown old, avarice alone flourishes]. Bromyard's explanation of this fact is novel, but symptomatic. He notes that as a man more eagerly clutches his own goods when other men come near him, so does an old man amass temporal goods when he sees many men like him who are nearing death and the loss of their goods. Chaucer himself, in the Reeve's Prologue, specifically links old age and avarice:

> Foure gleedes han we, which I shal devyse,—
> Avauntyng, liyng, anger, coveitise;

Thise foure sparkles longen unto eelde.

(ll. 3883–85)

It seems natural enough, then, that Chaucer chose to make this man old. But in doing so, Chaucer also realized how powerful the associations that would accompany such a figure would be. No longer just a repentant miser, the Old Man becomes an archetype, a reminder to every man who covets wealth that terrible beyond measure is the affliction this sin brings against the soul. For the Old Man has wandered to the ends of the earth seeking expiation for his sin, and with it the peace of Death. And as of now, he has not found it. But this changes before our eyes, for even the object of the Old Man's search, the exchange of youth for old age, may be seen in terms of avarice. For if longevity is one of the vice's qualities, this does not mean that the young are therefore immune: *Avaritia enim non parcit seni nec iuveni.* In the young rioters I think the Old Man finds three who *figuratively* would exchange their youthful desire for his former passion. Thus we might see the Old Man as a distinguished player in an ancient drama, an expiation myth which requires some sort of exchange to effect the protagonist's release. In Chaucer's version, expiation is wedded to Christian notions of repentance, satisfaction, and understanding. We see the Old Man at the moment of exchange and release; it is a timeless moment that recurs whenever the soul is struck by greed. The Old Man is perfectly honest with rioters and readers alike; what separates us from them is our greater understanding of his words. Death, Old Age, no matter what signification we assign him, the Old Man should be seen within the context of Chaucer's sermon on avarice. He is a figure who delights, who instructs, but who most of all leaves very few unmoved. He is a different guide, another text, from the Pardoner.

This essay has dealt with the Pardoner and the telling of his Tale. As a preacher who scorns God, the Pardoner lacks spiritual insight, and therefore is excessively literal. His inspiration is his own, and the conclusion of the Tale vividly demonstrates how his inspiration fails. Like the Old Man, the Pardoner is a victim of the sin of avarice; unlike the Old Man, the Pardoner remains defiant. He is a remarkable figure in a remarkable Tale, one that will continue to delight and puzzle us the more we understand.

"Synne Horrible":
The Pardoner's Exegesis of His Tale, and Chaucer's

H. Marshall Leicester, Jr.

To my mind the Canterbury tale that responds best to patristic or Augustinian forms of analysis is the Pardoner's. Such studies as that of R. P. Miller, showing the relevance to the tale of the tradition of the scriptural eunuch and the sin of presumption, or those of B. F. Huppé and Lee W. Patterson, demonstrating the even greater importance of the complementary sin of despair, are genuinely helpful in elucidating a narrative so patently, though at times so puzzlingly, allegorical. At the same time, as everyone knows, the tale is one of the most fully dramatized, the most "fitted to its teller" of any in the Canterbury collection. It has appealed to dramatically inclined critics from Kittredge on as an example of what is freshest and most untraditional in Chaucer's art. It would be disingenuous of me to attempt to conceal my own bias in favor of the latter kind of criticism, but I think there is something to be gained from attending carefully to the typological elements of the tale, because they are instructive about Chaucer's own attitude toward exegetical methods.

While no one can really deny, since Robertson's studies, that Chaucer uses these methods—at least sometimes—there has been a considerable reluctance by a great many critics to allow the implications that patristically influenced commentators tend to draw from this fact. I take E. T. Donaldson's comment, published seven years after the appearance of Robertson's "Doctrine of Charity in Medieval

From *Acts of Interpretation: The Text in Its Contexts 700–1600: Essays on Medieval and Renaissance Literature in Honor of E. Talbot Donaldson.* © 1982 by Pilgrim Books.

Literary Gardens" and five years before *A Preface to Chaucer,* as typical of a dissatisfaction that has continued unabated, despite the increasing number of detailed, and often attractive, demonstrations of the presence of typological elements in the poet's work:

> in my criticism I have been reluctant to invoke historical data from outside the poem to explain what is in it. . . . I have therefore eschewed the historical approach used both by the great Chaucerians of the earlier part of this century and by those scholars who have recently been reading Chaucer primarily as an exponent of medieval Christianity. The fact that the difference between what these two historical approaches have attained is absolute—if Chaucer means what the older Chaucerians thought he meant he cannot possibly mean what these newer Chaucerians think he means—has encouraged me to rely on the poems as the principal source of their meaning.

Perhaps one reason for critical hesitation has been the rather illiberal tone of much patristic criticism, tending to insist as it does that most really interesting human activities are, from a medieval perspective, no more or less than sins. To object to this tone is to risk dismissal as a historically conditioned sentimentalist, but I think that what really lies behind the objection is the feeling that if the exegetical critics are right our ancestors were, in their well-documented distrust of poetry, an impossibly reductive lot, unable to distinguish clearly between a daisy of the field and the Virgin Mary, and (perhaps rightly) preferred to see the latter whenever they encountered the former.

Still, in the Pardoner's Tale, these so-called historical elements are stubbornly present. It helps a lot to know something about a tradition of interpretation based on the idea that, while men make words stand for things, God can make things themselves stand for other things, in dealing with what is being communicated by a passage like the following (lines 350–65):

> Thanne have I in latoun a sholder-boon
> Which that was of an hooly Jewes sheep.
> "Goode men," I seye, "taak of my wordes keep;
> If that this boon be wasshe in any welle,
> If cow, or calf, or sheep, or oxe swelle
> That any worm hath ete, or worm ystonge,

Taak water of that welle and wassh his tonge,
And it is hool anon; and forthermoore,
Of pokkes and of scabbe, and every soore
Shal every sheep be hool that of this welle
Drynketh a draughte. Taak kep eek what I telle:
If that the good-man that the beestes oweth
Wol every wyke, er that the cok hym croweth,
Fastynge, drynken of this welle a draughte,
As thilke hooly Jew oure eldres taughte,
His beestes and his stoor shal multiplie."

(F. N. Robinson, 2d ed.)

At the literal level this specimen of the Pardoner's "gaude" is a blatant appeal to the cupidity, or at any rate to the decidedly secular interests, of his "lewed" audience. The bone is a kind of snake oil. Yet the imagery the Pardoner uses about and around the supposed relic—sheep, holy Jews, devouring worms, life-giving wells—seems insistently to imply much more. I do not think it is forcing the passage at all to see in it a persistent typological edge characteristic of his style. The fundamental link the passage takes advantage of is the equation between sheep and Christian souls, the helpless beasts endangered by the worm that dieth not, whom the Good Shepherd has in care. Accordingly, the ancient holy Jew takes on associations with Jacob, perhaps (via the well), and almost certainly with the promise to Abraham echoed in the last line quoted (Gen. 22:16–18). This in turn implies a complex and sophisticated series of interpretations of that promise, originally applied literally to and by the children of Israel under the Old Law, but since figurally fulfilled at a spiritual level under the New Law in the care of Christ for his flock. This fulfillment is presently embodied in the Pardoner's own profession and act, the salvation of souls by the mercy of Christ, mediated through the *plenitudo potestatis* of the papacy and the agency of the man before us. I am being deliberately impressionistic rather than "textueel" here, because what I want to establish is not a particular exegesis but that a spiritual level of meaning is being deliberately and consciously put in play by the speaker behind and around the literal offer of worldly "heele" and enrichment. It seems to me that the passage is overloaded in the direction of this kind of spiritual significance. There is something gratuitous not about the reading itself but about the Pardoner's insistence on packing it in in the very act of mocking and debasing it with his pitch. It is one thing to announce that you are a fraud and that you intend, though unrepentant, to expose your own fraudulent arts. It is another thing to load those arts themselves with a set of under meanings that exhibit so complex an awareness of the truth you are abusing. The Pardoner seems to be saying not only "look how I deceive the ignorant" but also "look at what an important matter I deceive them about." Whatever his motives for this, it is at least clear that the effect is achieved by a deliberate forcing of mundane and particular matters into a general and spiritual framework while at the same time refusing to let go of the literal level, so that we see both significances at the same time and are unsure to which one to assign priority. I think most readers will agree that much of the power of the Pardoner's Tale as a whole derives from a consistent application of this method to the materials of the story. A good deal of the eeriness of the Pardoner's central exemplum, for example, comes from the fact that it reverses the invariable order of causes found in all of its analogues, from *The Arabian Nights* to *The Treasure of the Sierra Madre*. In those stories the gold always comes first, and the point is to show that in looking for gold men find death. But in the Pardoner's Tale we *begin* with a search for death and find the gold later. The Pardoner's version thrusts the spiritual implications of the quest into the situation at the outset and juxtaposes them sharply to the extreme, childlike literal-mindedness of the three rioters, who treat death like a bully from the next town.

I intend to argue that such a failure or refusal to distinguish carefully and consistently between literal and spiritual levels of meaning and discourse is at the center of the Pardoner's Tale, the single most important determinant of the tale's meaning, and that the source of this effect is the consciousness of the Pardoner himself. The Pardoner is, I will further argue, the first exegetical critic of his own tale, obsessed with the spiritual meanings he sees beneath the surface of everyday life. He feels the burden of these meanings himself and attempts, as we shall see, to impose them on others. The Pardoner has long been recognized as the most self-conscious of the Canterbury pilgrims. Part of that self-consciousness involves an awareness of his own condition, and by this I do not mean simply that he attempts to hide his physical eunuchry, since I am not at all sure that he does. The Pardoner's conduct of his tale indicates that among the things he knows about himself and is concerned to make others see are the things R. P. Miller knows about him: that he is the *eunuchus non dei*, the embodiment of the *vetus homo*, the Old Man whose body is the body of this death, and guilty of the sin against the Holy Ghost.

II

From the very beginning there is something conspicuous and aggressive about the Pardoner's failure to conceal his various evils and deficiencies, well before he "confesses" some of them in his tale. The general narrator, the Host, and the "gentils" all see through him at once, and it seems likely that they can do so because the Pardoner makes it easy for them. A. C. Spearing has pointed to the obvious fakery of his authorizing bulls from popes and cardinals, and Kellogg and Haselmayer report that the abuse of carrying *false* relics is "so rare that no contemporary manual even discusses it." Since the relics themselves—pillowcases and pigs' bones—convince no one, we have the impression that this particular Pardoner goes out of his way to stage his abuses and make them even more blatant than those of most of his historically attested compeers. The same is true of his physical and sexual peculiarities. I take it that such things as his immediate echoing of the Host's "manly" oath "by Seint Ronyan" and his announced preference for jolly wenches in every town though babies starve for it have in common the tactic of calling attention to his oddity by deliberately shamming exaggerated virility. This is a form of camp, in which the hypermasculinity is as fully in quotes as the mock demonism of what Patterson calls his "gross and deliberate parody of sinfulness." The Pardoner's manner *courts* an interpretation that his confession simply confirms and heightens, and what interests me most is that the consistent drift of the interpretation he suggests is theological in character. His prologue continually circles back to typologically charged images like the dove sitting on a barn of line 397, or more direct comparisons such as "I wol noon of the apostles countrefete" (l. 447). Although the performance here may be interpreted as a joke, the humor derives from the disproportion between the ultimate issues that are constantly being raised and the cheap faker who raises them—and it is the Pardoner himself who keeps pointing up the discrepancy.

Nor is it clear, even at this early stage, that the Pardoner is only joking. He seems obscurely troubled that his performances can

" 'maken oother folk to twynne / From avarice, and soore to repente' " (ll. 430–31), and, as Patterson has pointed out, he insists somewhat too strongly that he does it only for the money. His oddly serious warning about the dangers of false preaching (ll. 407–22) reveals how the act has a complexity for him that belies his insistence that he himself preaches only for gain and "al by rote." If we try to deduce the motives that his own sermon reveals in its unfolding, these more serious aspects of the Pardoner's self-presentation—what he wants us to see about himself and the world—begin to come clearer.

The sermon provides an intense, almost hallucinatory vision of a world dominated and consumed by sin, in which gluttony "Maketh that est and west and north and south, / In erthe, in eir, in water, men to swynke / To gete a glotoun deyntee mete and drynke" (ll. 518–20). The feeling that sin is everywhere, and everywhere having its effect on the world, is heightened by the tendency to assimilate the effects of all sins to each individual sin, and to combine sins together (ll. 591–94):

> Hasard is verray mooder of lesynges,
> And of deceite, and cursed forswerynges,
> Blaspheme of Crist, manslaughtre, and wast also
> Of catel and of tyme.

Such passages in isolation might simply be considered exaggeration appropriate to any preacher striving to move his hearers to repentance. But the Pardoner's way of exaggerating is more complicated. It is one thing to say, as both the Parson and the Pardoner do, that the world was corrupted by gluttony, or to say that original sin contained all other sins in itself potentially. It is quite another thing to say that the original sin was gluttony (ll. 508–11). A standard theological point is turned around here by deliberately overliteralizing the spiritual interrelation of all sins to one another, in keeping with the general tendency of the sermon to treat matter rather than spirit as the root of all evil: "O wombe! O bely! O stynkyng cod, / Fulfilled of dong and of corrupcioun!" (ll. 534–35).

It is clear enough that the Pardoner hates his body and the flesh in general. He consistently and gratuitously forces details that express disgust at the corruption of the physical, from his description of his reliquaries "ycrammed ful of cloutes and of bones" (l. 348) to the sheep that need healing, "Of pokkes and of scabbe, and every soore" (l. 358) to the brilliant way we are brought too close to the drunkard: "sour is thy breeth, *foul artow to embrace*" (l. 552). Especially in the description of gluttony, but also elsewhere in the sermon, the Pardoner moves well beyond mere asceticism to an obsessive insistence on the brutal and ugly condition of the flesh, and especially of its *burden,* the sheer labor of keeping this death-bound and filthy bag alive: "How greet labour and cost is thee to fynde!" (l. 537). This kind of thing gives a peculiarly literal (and powerful) emphasis to the frequent and quite orthodox refrain that sin is a living death and that the sinner "Is deed, whil that he lyveth in tho vices" (l. 548, cf. ll. 533, 558).

I do not think, however, that this sense of physical corruption, weakness, and impotence is at the root of the Pardoner's character and problem, any more than I think that he wishes to conceal his own physical impotence. It should be noted that the ascription of the Fall to gluttony is funny, and deliberately so. It gets its effect from taking the stock rant of "Corrupt was al this world for glotonye" (l. 504) and treating it as if it were literally true, and the Pardoner's qualifying asides ("it is no drede," "as I rede") show that he knows this, that he is parodying a certain sort of preaching at the same time that he is doing it. Such parodying of sermon styles is satirical, a mocking condemnation of the inadequacy of literal forms and institutions to contain or even define the reality of sin, and the Pardoner does it throughout his sermon (ll. 639–47):

> Bihoold and se that in the firste table
> Of heighe Goddes heestes honurable,
> Hou that the seconde heeste of hym is this:
> "Take nat my name in ydel or amys."
> Lo, rather he forbedeth swich sweryng
> Than homycide or many a cursed thyng;
> I seye that, as by ordre, thus it stondeth;
> This knoweth, that his heestes understondeth,
> How that the seconde heeste of God is that.

This passage makes fun of a style of thinking and moralizing whose literalness renders it preposterous. It pursues classification, labeling, and external order at the expense of clear ethical priorities and gives us an image of the preacher as a demented scholastic. A complementary figure is Stilboun, the "wys embassadour," who is himself a moralist and a preacher but also a Johnny One-note who can only nag over and over that his principals "Shul nat allyen yow with hasardours" (l. 618, cf. ll. 613, 616). I think the Pardoner means these various examples, and the entire sermon, as comments on the kind of preaching, theology, and pastoral care that goes on in the church he represents. Even the snake-oil pitch to the "lewed peple" with which I began uses its typological elements to juxtapose and contrast what pardoning ought to be doing with what it actually does. We are so used to thinking of the Pardoner as an *embodiment* of the notorious abuses of the fourteenth-century church that we tend not to consider that he has *attitudes* toward them. But his parodic presentation of doctrinal classification, moral exhortation, and religious institutions like the cult of relics and pardoning itself consistently suggests his contempt for the available instruments of salvation as they are used in the real life of the all-too-corporeal *corpus mysticum* around him. He is in fact a *proponent* of the older historical view of the tale as a satire on the corruption of the church. The satire is the Pardoner's, and his own best example is himself.

This last is important. One of the striking rhetorical features of the entire sermon is the way it keeps associating all the sins it describes with the Pardoner—showing that he is guilty of them. The most striking instances of this tendency are the passages where the Pardoner demonstrates his experienced familiarity with the sins he purports to condemn, as in the description of the drunken dice game (ll. 651–55) that Donaldson calls "so knowingly graphic as to exceed the limits of art," or the discussion of abuses of the wine trade and the difficulty of getting an honest drink (ll. 562–72). There is nothing concealed or private about the Pardoner's complicity in these vices; rather, he brings himself forward as an instance of them, and this reflexive element gives a particular bite and appropriateness to the concentration in the sermon on the increased sinfulness and conse-quentiality of sin in high places. "A capitayn sholde lyve in sobre-nesse" (l. 582), but this one does not, as he shows. Given the context, who else can the Pardoner be talking about here? "Redeth the Bible, and fynde it expresly / Of wyn-yevyng to hem that han justise" (l. 587), or (ll. 595–98):

> It is repreeve and contrarie of honour
> For to ben holde a commune hasardour.
> And ever the hyer he is of estaat,
> The moore is he yholden desolaat.

All these images are in effect types and figures of the Pardoner himself, and he in turn is a type and figure of everything about the church—its institutions, its preaching, its corrupt ministers—that fails to come to grips with the reality of sin in the world. That reality is, as I have already suggested, very real to the Pardoner. He portrays the wretchedness and misery of the human condition with immediacy and insight. He demonstrates how traditional patterns of classification, description, and exhortation fail to catch or contain the more intimate and existential presence of sin, death, and the burden of the flesh which he sees in others and feels in himself. He has nothing but contempt, and this in a deeper sense than we have yet examined, for the consolations of religion, but he takes very seriously the things they are intended to console. On the one hand there is the horror of life; on the other there is the church that fails to address or ameliorate that horror—a dead letter, and one that kills. Caught between them and embodying them both is the Pardoner (ll. 530–33):

> Ther walken manye of whiche yow toold have I—
> I seye it now wepyng, with pitous voys—
> That they been enemys of Cristes croys,
> Of whiche the ende is deeth.

The emphasis in the sermon section of the tale divides fairly evenly between these two perspectives (though both are always present), on either side of our most immediate and least hyper-rhetorical view of him, the passage on the wine of Fish Street and Cheapside. Before that he tends primarily to develop his heightened view of life's ugliness and the universality of sin. After it he concentrates more on the self-condemning mockery of the forms of religious ministry. This division points to and helps explain the development of the Pardoner's consciousness in the tale, the way something *happens* to him here. What happens is that, as he manipulates the conventional materials of the sermon to reflect his own obsessions, he becomes more conscious of himself and more aware of both his power and his powerlessness. The power derives from the way he makes himself into a symbol, generalizes his own sinful and death-bound condition to the world around him. He makes the extent and the seriousness of what he stands for (what he *makes* himself stand for) more explicit as he dramatizes the evil God cannot or will not eliminate. His own presumption, for that is what it is, has the power of making a wasteland of the world. His powerlessness derives from the fact that what he symbolizes (what he *makes* himself symbolize) is emptiness and privation. His despair, for that is what it is, makes his inability to save others or himself the most salient fact of existence.

Cupiditas, of course, means far more than avarice. In the deep Christian and Augustinian sense in which it is the contrary of *caritas,* it refers to a consuming desire for that which one is lacking—it means *wanting* in both senses, or rather, wanting in a particular way. Privation itself is a fundamental fact of the human condition. Saint Augustine images it as the state of a pilgrim far from the blessedness of his home (*De doctrina* 1.4.4). Given this basic lack, two responses are possible. To use (*utor*) the things of this world as a way to get beyond them to God is, paradoxically, to grant them their independence, to open up the possibility of using them in charity, of cherishing them (*De doctrina* 1.33.37). The enjoyment (*fruor*) of the world and others which is *cupiditas* only looks like enjoying them for their own sakes—it really means wanting to enjoy them for oneself, to engulf them and make them the instruments of one's own will. In traditional terms, despair *is* presumption: to say that God cannot forgive you is to place limits on His power and mercy, to usurp a judgment that belongs to Him. In its largest sense *cupiditas* is the desire to do this, and its inevitable frustration produces the hatred of God, self, and others that the Pardoner displays. This is the condition that the Pardoner suffers and wills. It is the condition that he half conceals or avoids in the Prologue and that he *embodies* in the sermon. The extent to which his despair breaks loose in the sermon is indicated by the notorious fact that he forgets at the end of it that he has not yet told us how many rioters there are. I interpret this as a sign of the extent to which he has become caught up in the sermon, lost control of the form of his tale in the act of dramatizing his condition, the universality of that condition, and its effects in the world. It is this heightened consciousness that he carries into the exemplum he is at last ready to tell.

III

The exemplum itself is not well fitted to express the Pardoner's view of things. It is hard to imagine that any exemplum would be, since the form itself is an example of the institutionalized literalism he despises. The traditional form of the Pardoner's exemplum argues the proposition "If you are avaricious you will die" in the most literal, and therefore unbelievable way. It presents a clarified picture of the operations of divine justice that both the Pardoner's experience and his very existence utterly deny. The exemplum is precisely one of those worthless forms of spiritual teaching, too far removed from the reality of life and sin, that the Pardoner mocks in his sermon. This is one reason he modifies the early parts of the exemplum in the way he does, in an attempt to get the letter of the story to express something about spirit, and the well-attested oddness of the resulting effect shows the inaptness of the form to the purpose.

The peculiarities of the Pardoner's telling are gathered around and focus on the Old Man. The first part of the tale is, in fact, designed to prepare a context for him, and that is why it brings death into the foreground. It has become fairly commonplace by now to see the three rioters and the Old Man as aspects of the Pardoner, and I agree with this notion in general. The problem remains, however, of situating this division in the consciousness of the Pardoner himself, of seeing how he uses it and what he uses it to say. The feeling of miasma in the opening scene arises, as I have previously suggested, from the semi-allegorical treatment of an ordinary tavern scene in such a way as to stress its spiritual overtones (ll. 670–84; emphasis mine):

> "Sire," quod this boy, "it nedeth never-a-deel;
> It was me toold er ye cam heer two houres.
> He was, pardee, *an old felawe of youres;*
> And sodeynly he was yslayn to-nyght,
> Fordronke, as he sat on his bench upright.
> Ther came a privee theef man clepeth Deeth,
> That *in this contree* al the peple sleeth,
> And with his spere he smoot his herte atwo,
> And went his way withouten wordes mo.
> He hath a thousand slayn this pestilence.
> And, maister, *er ye come in his presence,*
> *Me thynketh that it were necessarie*
> *For to be war of swich an adversarie.*
> *Beth redy for to meete him everemoore;*
> Thus taughte me my dame; I sey namoore."

The italicized phrases outline points at which the Pardoner's sophisticated typological consciousness imposes on the innocent one of the youth. Because of what is at issue, "felawe" points to the fellowship of all men in sin and before death, "this contree" moves toward "this world," and the final warning urges the need for a different kind of readiness and preparation from what the boy seems to have in mind. And who is "my dame"? Nature? The church? The child speaks more than he knows.

At one level these characters are an image of the Pardoner's audience, of the "lewed peple" who live in ignorant literal-mindedness in a world that is more charged with spiritual significance and consequence than they can imagine. They treat reality as if it were an exemplum and respond to the offense against human integrity, self-sufficiency, and community that death is ("Er that he dide a man a dishonour," l. 691), as to an external threat, an isolated event, something merely physical. It has also become common of late to point out that the rioters' quest is a blasphemous parody of Christ's sacrifice, which slew spiritual death for the faithful once and for all. This is true, and it is another instance of the typological processing that the Pardoner goes out of his way to give the tale. But it also seems to me that he regards this aspect of the rioters with a certain ambivalence, even sympathy. There is something attractive in the youthful idealism that so confidently forms a band of brothers to slay death. The rioters do not seem really evil in the early parts of the tale; they are too innocent for that. A student of mine once compared them to fraternity boys, as much for their trivial dissipation as for their idealism, and the Pardoner's earliest characterization of their lives is not "sin" but "folye" (l. 464). I think he is momentarily attracted to their quest because it does correspond to something in him, and was once his own. What once must have been a desire to do "Cristes hooly werk," to slay death and save souls by offering them Christ's pardon, is nostalgically revived in the rioter's quest and at the same time placed as naive and overconfident folly. The rioters, as once perhaps the Pardoner, have no idea what they are up against.

What they are up against is the Old Man, the truth of the experience of the *vetus homo* as that experience is embodied in the consciousness of the Pardoner. He is what their quest leads to, and what they might become if they did not live in an exemplum. The Pardoner uses the Old Man as a spokesman for this sophisticated despair. The Old Man's desire to exchange age for youth (ll. 720–26) points to the Pardoner's envy of the innocence of the rioters and of his "lewed" congregation and suggests that what he wants to be rid of is not physical decay but consciousness. Although he sounds suicidal (ll. 727–33), the Old Man is not so in the ordinary sense. Because he feels himself eternal, physical death is beside the point. What he wants is to be swallowed up, to become nothing, to escape from the restless *consciousness* of his privation, his *cupiditas*. This is that sickness unto death of which Kierkegaard speaks, "everlastingly to die, to die and yet not to die, to die the death."

To wish to exchange one's chest for a hair shirt (ll. 734–38) is, in effect and typologically, to wish to be able to pay money for the gift of repentance, to wish that the literal version of pardoning were the true one. Besides demonstrating decisively that avarice is not at issue here, this indicates that the Pardoner understands that his situation is willed. He would have to repent to get any relief, and he *will* not, though he knows this is the source of his wretchedness. He also knows what this makes him (ll. 739–47):

> "But, sires, to yow it is no curteisye
> To speken to an old man vileynye,
> But he trespasse in word, or elles in dede.
> In Hooly Writ ye may yourself wel rede:
> 'Agayns an oold man, hoor upon his heed,
> Ye sholde arise;' wherfore I yeve yow reed,
> Ne dooth unto an oold man noon harm now,
> Namoore than that ye wolde men did to yow
> In age, if that ye so longe abyde."

This passage, like the rest of the Old Man's speech, is the place in the tale where the Pardoner most clearly expresses his self-pity. But his language also shows that he understands his condition spiritually and exegetically, that he *interprets himself* in traditional terms as the *vetus homo*. This makes the self-pity begin to shade over into the self-hatred that is its complement. The Pardoner's voicing of the unambiguous passage from Leviticus makes it move toward self-condemnation—from "respect your elders" to "rise up against an Old Man." This is especially clear if the speech is taken where it belongs, outside the tale and in relation to the Pardoner, who goes so far out of his way to show how he trespasses in word and deed.

The encounter with the Old Man is the place in the tale where the Pardoner most openly discloses his own condition. It is the place where we feel the least sense of the detachment of his voice from the surface of the story, the least irony and manipulation. It is the point at which he completes the process of putting himself into his tale, and the apparent result is that he has nowhere to go. The Old Man can point the way to death, but as soon as he does so he vanishes from the story "thider as I have to go" (l. 749). The rioters cannot hear what the Old Man has to tell them, that physical death is only a figure for the spiritual, for something that is eternally within them and in which they live without knowing it. They can only enact the literal and mechanical poetic justice of an exemplum about avarice—or so it seems. Although there is some truth to the idea that the tale becomes more narrow and limited and loses much of its atmosphere of mystery after the departure of the Old Man, it seems to me that his pointing finger remains to haunt the tale in the "signes and othere circumstances" the Pardoner imposes on the simple exemplum plot.

On the one hand he traces the psychological progress of the rioters. Their idealism quickly flips over into its contrary and generates a world of cynicism and suspicion in which "Men wolde seyn that we were theves stronge, / And for oure owene tresor doon us honge" (ll. 789–90), and every man's hand is against every other's. This suggests the basic sense of the world that generated the idealism, the impulse to kill death, in the first place, and so identifies the underlying protodespair of the rioters. This is seen most clearly in the youngest, whose decision to murder his fellows is presented as an accession of self-consciousness. Like his companions he begins with a heightened awareness of the beauty of the world ("thise floryns newe and bryghte," l. 839, cf. ll. 773–74) that distracts him from brotherhood and the quest for death. This quickly shades into *cupiditas,* the desire to possess the object beheld for himself, in order to complete an existence suddenly perceived as lacking (ll. 840–43):

> "O Lord!" quod he, "if so were that I myghte
> Have al this tresor to myself allone,
> Ther is no man that lyveth under the trone
> Of God that sholde lyve so murye as I!"

The account of how the fiend suggested to him that he should buy poison is theologically careful, not for the sake of the theological point but in order to point up a shift from external temptation to an inner motion of the will that discovers the preexisting depravity of the soul: "For-why the feend foond hym in swich lyvynge / That he hadde leve him to sorwe brynge" (ll. 847–48). By the time the youngest rioter gets to the apothecary, his imagery has begun to resonate with that despairing sense of wasting away that is the Pardoner's own: "And fayn he wolde wreke hym, if he myghte, / On vermyn that destroyed hym by nyghte" (l. 858). The Pardoner seems to try to bring the rioters up to the point at which they might begin to discover the *vetus homo* or outcast the old Adam in themselves and so begin to share the consciousness of the Old Man.

At the same time the Pardoner plays with the imagery and structure of the tale so as to suggest in a different way what is "really" going on. His typological imagination seizes on certain details of the story in order to allude to the spiritual plot of the tale that its literal unfolding obscures. The "breed and wyn" (l. 797) that ultimately kill the rioters, whatever precise interpretation be put on them, are surely an example of a deliberate introduction of sacramental imagery. Similarly, the apothecary's description of the poison has the by now familiar overloaded quality of physical details forced onto a spiritual plane (ll. 859–64):

> The pothecarie answerde, "And thou shalt have
> A thyng that, also God my soule save,
> In al this world ther is no creature,
> That eten or dronken hath of this confiture
> Noght but the montance of a corn of whete,
> That he ne shal his lif anon forlete."

The reference, I take it, is to John 12:24: "Truly, truly, I say to you, unless a grain of wheat falls into the earth and dies it remains alone; but if it dies it bears much fruit. He who loves his life loses it, and he who hates his life in this world will keep it for eternal life." The standard commentaries identify the grain as the Eucharist by which the faithful soul ought to live and spiritual fruit to arise. Similarly, the "large botelles thre" (l. 871, cf. l. 877) which the youngest rioter fills with his poisoned wine refer to the saying of Jesus: "And no one puts new wine into old wineskins; if he does the wine will burst the skins and the wine is lost and so are the skins; but new wine is for fresh skins" (Mark 2:22; cf. Matt. 9:17, Luke 5:37). Jerome takes this as referring to the transition from the Old Law to the New. Until a man is reborn and puts aside the *vetus homo,* he cannot contain the new wine of the Gospel precepts. The *Glossa ordinaria,* following Bede, reads the wine as the Holy Spirit that transformed the apostles from old to new men but whose spiritual precepts destroy the scribes and Pharisees of the Old Law and the proud generally. Since in the story it is evident that the rioters must be the old bottles that are burst, the pattern of typological action in the tale seems clear and consistent: the New Law of Salvation, the Eucharist as the sacrifice of Christ, is poison to these *veteres homines.* This or something like it is the Pardoner's exegesis of the tale. The peculiarity of this exegesis—it is hardly usual to present the instruments of Christ's mercy as poison—reflects the Pardoner's own experience of the promise of salvation and his more spiritual sense of himself as the Old Man. At the literal level, as it applies to the rioters, the justice of the tale has a certain Old Testament savagery, but how much worse to alienate oneself from a loving and merciful God who lays down His own life for man's sins. It is this that makes what poisons the rioters literally a spiritual poison to the Pardoner: it heightens his sense of what he has cut himself off from.

IV

What is striking about all this psychological and theological sophistication, however, is how little effect it finally has on the exemplum. If in the course of his tale the Pardoner has embodied his sense of himself and the world and put his "venym under hewe of holynesse" into literal bottles of poisoned wine—spirituality under hue of venom as it were—that embodiment remains eccentric, sporadic, and largely veiled, more deeply felt by the Pardoner than argued in the story. The large-scale patterns of spiritual reference that critics have detected in the tale are all there, more or less, and they are there because the Pardoner puts them there, but they remain largely implicit and structural, carried by typological allusions to be caught only by the learned. Indeed, the very fact that the Pardoner makes the tale *more* typological as he proceeds shows his increasing sense that he cannot get it to say what he wants more directly. One feels that he is trying to make the story bear more weight than it comfortably can, to push its symbolic significance too far.

It seems likely that the Pardoner feels the same way, for when he comes to what should be the rhetorical high point of the exemplum, the description of the death agonies of the rioters, he tosses it away with a "What nedeth it to sermone of it moore?" (l. 879) and a coolly toned reference to a medical textbook (ll. 889–95). I take the feeling of anticlimax here as an indication of the Pardoner's impatience with the conventional poetic justice of the ending. As it stands, the exemplum does not solve or settle anything he feels to be important. The rioters are gone, but sin, death, and the Pardoner remain (ll. 895–903):

> O cursed synne of all cursednesse!
> A traytours homycide, O wikkednesse!
> O glotonye, luxurie, and hasardrye!
> Thou blasphemour of Crist with vileynye
> And othes grete, of usage and of pride!
> Allas! mankynde, how may it bitide
> That to thy creatour, which that the wroghte,
> And with his precious herte-blood thee boghte,
> Thou art so fals and so unkynde, allas?

It is notable that this moralization of the exemplum, for all its appropriately heightened rhetorical tone, does not arise directly from the events of the tale and only arrives at the "right" moral ("ware yow fro the synne of avarice!" l. 905) after several lines of impassioned condemnation of "mankynde" for the same old tavern vices. These vices are generally appropriate to the occasion in the sense that the rioters are guilty of them, but their introduction here breaks the continuity and focus of the conclusion of the tale, and it is difficult to know what to make of the intensity with which they are denounced after the flat tone of the account of the rioters' demise. It is as if the Pardoner were looking for something on which to vent strong feelings and casting about for a pretext. What the passage does accomplish is a return of the image of a world pervaded by sin generated by the sermon section of the tale. Juxtaposed to this image, more directly and immediately than ever before, is the Pardoner's self-presentation, which bitterly and cynically compares his mercenary activity (on which he harps) with what it is supposed to pardon (ll. 904–15).

Throughout the tale it has been the Pardoner's explicit project to make an example of himself, to unmask and explain his practices. In the course of the telling, as I have tried to show, his *attitude* toward himself and his profession, his self-hatred and self-condemnation, coupled as always with his hatred and contempt of others, has emerged with increasing clarity and intensity, at least for him. His

self-presentation throughout the tale constantly stresses his culpabil-
ity, and as the tale proceeds, he seems to tkae this with increasing
seriousness, to regard himself as truly exemplary and symbolic of the
evil, corruption, and sinfulness of the world—finally, perhaps, as a
type of the Antichrist. I have been at pains to show that what
exegetical criticism detects in the tale and makes an external doctrinal
structure that contains and explains a Pardoner unaware of it is in fact
the Pardoner's interpretation of himself, consciously undertaken and
offered by him to the pilgrims. It is only when the action of the tale
is understood in this way that the epilogue begins to make sense.

By the end of the story the Pardoner seems dominated by his
tale: he rejects it at a literal level but remains racked by the
heightened and frustrated consciousness of himself that the experience of telling it generates in him. This leads him to force the issues
of sin and spirit, the issue of himself, beyond the tale itself into the
real world of the pilgrimage. The real moral the Pardoner has come
to draw from the real exemplum of the tale, himself, emerges as he
completes that exemplum (ll. 915–18):

> And lo, sires, thus I preche.
> And Jhesu Crist, that is oure soules leche,
> So graunte yow his pardoun to receyve,
> For that is best; I wol yow nat deceyve.

These famous lines represent not a "paroxysm of agonized sincerity"
suddenly arrived at but a simple and direct statement of half of what
the Pardoner has been saying all along. They take their full energy
here only from the presentation of the other half which immediately
follows. "What you need is Christ's pardon—what you get is mine"
(ll. 919–45):

> But, sires, o word forgat I in my tale:
> I have relikes and pardoun in my male,
> As faire as any man in Engelond,
> Which were me yeven by the popes hond.
> If any of yow wole, of devocion,
> Offren, and han myn absolucion,
> Com forth anon, and kneleth heere adoun,
> And mekely receyveth my pardoun;
> Or elles taketh pardoun as ye wende,
> Al newe and fressh at every miles ende,

So that ye offren, alwey newe and newe,
Nobles or pens, whiche that be goode and trewe.
It is an honour to everich that is heer
That ye mowe have a suffisant pardoneer
T'assoile yow, in contree as ye ryde,
For aventures whiche that may bityde.
Paraventure ther may fallen oon or two
Doun of his hors, and breke his nekke atwo.
Looke which a seuretee is it to yow alle
That I am in youre felaweshipe yfalle,
That may assoille yow, bothe moore and lasse,
Whan that the soule shal fro the body passe.
I rede that oure Hoost heere shal bigynne,
For he is moost enveluped in synne.
Com forth, sire Hoost, and offre first anon,
And thou shalt kisse the relikes everychon,
Ye, for a grote! Unbokele anon thy purs.

When these lines are read in context, it is hard to match them anywhere in Chaucer for sheer venom. There is direct venom against the pilgrims, to be sure—"Paraventure ther may fallen oon or two" sounds like a wish—but most of his contempt for them arises from their failure to see and respond to what the Pardoner here says he is. The passage recapitulates in concentrated form all the aggressive methods of dramatized self-condemnation the Pardoner has used throughout the tale—his conspicuous avarice, his ridiculous bulls, his rag-and-bone "relics," even the hints of perverse sexuality in the obscene invitation of "unbokele anon thy purs"—and tries to ram them down the pilgrims' throats. It does so, moreover, in such a way as to give greatest stress to the symbolic significance of these offered insults. Over and over the speech says: "I am what the pope licenses, what the church supplies for your spiritual needs. I am the instrument of Christ's mercy, the representative of the Holy Ghost among you. I am what you kneel to, whose relics you kiss. I am that *cupiditas* which is the root of evils, the Old Adam, the obscenity of the *eunuchus non dei* that invites to fruitless generation. See what I make of the instruments of salvation. What do *you* make of a church that licenses me, of a world in which I am possible, of a God that allows me to exist?" This too is what the Pardoner has been saying all along. As an instance of what Kierkegaard calls the demoniac form of despair, the Pardoner posits himself as a malignant *objection* to God and his creation. He presents himself as a proof against the goodness of existence and wills his own misery and evil as a protest against God; he forces into the open what was before only implicit in his self-dramatization, trying to *make* the pilgrims see it. This, finally, is what lies behind the Pardoner's typologizing of himself. His consistent practice is to convert the literal, the everyday, the phenomenal, to a sign for spirit. This is his idealism, in the technical sense, and it accounts for the feeling his tale notoriously gives of a world in which the power of the word over reality is nearly total. Having made these transformations, he then insists that the spiritual meaning of an old man, a bottle, or a pardoner is what these things *are* and how they must be treated. This insistence is, in another sense, his literalism, his delusion. But this again is an expression of his own spiritual state, his presumption and despair. The Pardoner's greatest self-condemnation is his moment of greatest pride, the moment when he attempts to force upon the pilgrims his own symbolic, typological vision of himself. What he *wants* here is to get them to take this vision for reality.

What he gets, however, is a set of responses that measures his excess and places it in a world at once more real and more ordinary than the one he has constructed in the course of telling his tale. The Host's answer to the Pardoner's final speech contains touches that seem to recognize the latter's spiritual perspective and perhaps testify to its immediate rhetorical and emotional power: "Nay, nay!" quod he, "thanne have I Cristes curs!" (l. 946). But I think that what makes the already angry Pardoner even angrier—and silences him—is not that the Host "reveals" a sexual defect the Pardoner has been at pains to suggest and exploit but that Harry Bailly responds to a spiritual attack with a merely literal one. The Host's answer is not directed to the *eunuchus non dei,* only to a gelding. His response shows that he has missed the point of the Pardoner's self-presentation. His brutal literalism cuts through the tissue of spiritual allusion and moral self-dramatization in the Pardoner's final speech, reducing the Pardoner, his relics, and his "coillons," if he has them, to mere matter, and matter which is not even blasphemous, only insulting. The Host's explosion begins to restore a perspective which has been largely lost in the course of the tale's development when the Pardoner's voice is the only one before us—the perspective of the ordinary world.

There is a mood that sometimes comes on interpreters of the Pardoner's Tale in which the histrionics, pervasive irony, and symbolic pretension of the tale, the way it reaches for deep and ultimate meanings, seem open to skepticism: "*Isn't* it, after all, just a piece of entertainment? Isn't the end just a joke, isn't the Pardoner just a fund-raiser?" This way of viewing the tale is valuable because it pinpoints the distinction the tale as a whole makes between the Pardoner's idea of himself—the way he presents himself—and a more detached and balanced view. This is the view taken by the end of the poem, and associated with the community of the pilgrims, society. Harry Bailly may not know exactly what the Pardoner is doing, but he can tell that it is more than a joke, and at first he responds in kind to its aggressive violence, what he rightly calls its anger: he can feel that the Pardoner is imposing something on him. After his initial outburst, however, the Host begins to put the situation in perspective. He is obviously a little shaken by his own reaction, the extent to which he has been drawn in to the Pardoner's mood, and begins to back off: "I wol no lenger pleye / With thee, ne with noon oother angry man" (ll. 958–59). At this point other social forces intervene to break the mood further and to contain it, as the Knight, observing that "al the peple lough" (l. 961), urges a reconciliation: " 'as we diden, lat us laughe and pleye.' / Anon they kiste, and ryden forth hir weye" (ll. 967–68).

The conclusion of the tale frames the Pardoner's performance as a social gaffe, a joke in bad taste that has gotten out of hand. It does so by showing us how society closes ranks to repair the breach in decorum, the violation of the tale-telling contract the Pardoner has committed. The kiss of peace at the end is, of course, hollow, a mere social form that lets things move forward smoothly. It allows the group to pretend that nothing untoward has happened and leaves the Pardoner in frustrated possession of his unhappy consciousness. This may well increase our sympathy for him, but the group is nonetheless correct in its assessment of the situation, for the most effective criticism of the Pardoner's presumption is precisely that it is presumptuous in an ordinary sense. It is preposterous that any man should carry the symbolic weight the Pardoner gives himself. If he takes all our sins on his shoulders by committing them, scapegoats himself like Christ in order to dramatize the pervasive presence of spirit in ordinary life, this is likely to make us reflect that Christ did not do this out of self-hatred and that not everyone who climbs upon a cross is Christ or a type of Christ or even a type of Antichrist. Going only on New Testament probabilities, two out of three are likely to be common thieves.

The way the end of the tale is framed so as to bring the Pardoner's typological consciousness into contact with an actuality that contains him and reveals his limitations suggests that, far from being an example of Chaucer's belief in and commitment to typological methods, the tale as a whole represents the poet's *critique* of typology as a way of thinking about the world. We need to make a distinction between typological *methods,* which in Chaucer's practice are simply one set of rhetorical techniques among many and open to anyone who has a use for them, and a typological imagination. Chaucer uses the former occasionally (in fact rather rarely in his own voice in *The Canterbury Tales*), and he has various pilgrims use them for various purposes in their tales. Unlike Dante, however, he does not seem to have the latter. The Pardoner is the one pilgrim who really does seem to have a typological imagination, a mind that habitually views the smallest details of life in the world *sub specie aeternitatis,* and what Chaucer's presentation identifies is the violence this cast of mind does to experience. Because the Pardoner demands that the world must be more "perfect" in his own terms than it is, he is constrained to see and suffer it "out of alle charitee" as worse than it is, simpler, blacker, and less flexible. Chaucer, with his habitual awareness that there is no such thing as disinterested language, sees that even doctrine, as it is encountered in concrete life, did not fall from the sky but is always being used by someone for some end. From this perspective what the poet identifies in the Pardoner's Tale is the temptation to pride and the illusion of power that typological thinking encourages. He shows how such thinking may all too easily forget that it is only God who makes things themselves into signs for other things at the level of eternal truth. Chaucer's critique of typology identifies it as a potentially defective form of metaphor or image making that is too easily led to collapse the necessary distinctions between symbol and referent, literal and spiritual, mind and world. Less abstractly put, Chaucer shows that the Pardoner's tale is a bad *tale* because the Pardoner fails to see and sustain the crucial difference between fiction and reality, between a tale and the world in which it is told, and tries to force something he has made onto the world. The end of the tale shows that the typological imagination, by taking a God's-eye view, can all too easily deceive itself into playing God. This is a form of presumption that does not require divine intervention to discover its limitations.

The Pardoner is, as I have already suggested, the first exegetical critic of his own tale. He distorts his own sermon and exemplum by allegorizing and literalizing them beyond what they will bear. There is in this, perhaps, a lesson for much subsequent exegetical criticism, which, like the Pardoner himself, is too frequently docetist in tendency. That is, this kind of criticism often tends to imply that doctrine is more important than people, that the living temporal-historical experience of real souls has nothing to say for itself, or, typologically and symbolically put, that Christ could not really have deigned to sully his spirit, his divinity, by incarnating it in a real human person. This view is ultimately as unfair to Saint Augustine and the Middle Ages as it is to Chaucer. It can become a form of historical and critical pride, and it seems to me to be no accident that in its purest form exegetical criticism is associated with an attempt to cut off medieval consciousness from our common humanity, to say, for example, that "medieval man" (the generic reference is telling in this context) had no personality because "he" talked about it differently from the way we do. Such a view makes our ancestors simpler and purer, and therefore less human, than we are—or than they were. But I am beginning to sound like the Pardoner myself, and since I do not plan to burn Professor Robertson at the stake, let me say rather that exegetical criticism, if it loses its sense of proportion, can, like the Pardoner, get a little rude.

Chaucer's response, critical as it is of the typological imagination, is not simply a rejection of it but something far more complex and sympathetic. His attitude is not, or not only, that of the pilgrims who dismiss the Pardoner, close ranks, and "ryden forth hir weye"—after all, he wrote the tale. One frequently has the sense in *The Canterbury Tales* that audiences do not listen, that they do not hear what speakers are saying about themselves in their tales. In part, no doubt, this is a function of Chaucer's recognition of the important difference between real oral performance and the mediated literary imitation of oral telling he provides. No one could get out of a Canterbury tale what is in it by hearing it once, and by presenting the Pardoner's speaking in a written text—in the absence of the Pardoner himself and of the audience that dismissed him—Chaucer gives him more presence as a voice in the work than he apparently achieved on the pilgrimage. The fiction, perhaps, is that only Chaucer really understood the Pardoner and by writing him down gave him the chance to be read and reread—the chance to be heard.

This suggests that it is important to Chaucer that the Pardoner's voice *be* heard, in all its vividness, intensity, irony, and exegetical power. The reason for this, of course, is that the Pardoner is a considerable part of the poet. His impersonation of the Pardoner gives Chaucer a chance to exercise as well as exorcise his own attraction to the power of the poet's medium, language, over reality, and his fascination with the possibilities of typological symbolism. It also provides him with an opportunity to satirize the abuses of religious language he finds around him. Chaucer's first criticism of such speaking is surely the same as the Pardoner's: that it is too easily used to bolster and justify a corrupt establishment, to cover the ignorance, the lack of intelligence, and the moral obliquity of those who use it. The Pardoner speaks for the puritan, the utopian, the superior observer of human folly in Chaucer. There is too much truth (and too much fun) in the Pardoner's parody of sermons and exempla to think otherwise. The Pardoner's despair must also sometimes have been Chaucer's, or he could not have portrayed it so vividly. But Chaucer also sees what the Pardoner does not, the presumption of this attitude and the way it demands that God and the world conform to the impossible requirements of a human fantasy. The poet's own practice is counter to the Pardoner's; it consists in disciplining and subordinating his own vision to the portrayal of other consciousnesses, learning to see with the eyes and speak with the voices of others, to let the people, "lered oother lewed," speak for themselves. In the Pardoner's Tale, Chaucer both embodies and chastens his own impulse to play God, to judge and condemn his fellows and the world they all inhabit. The result of that chastening and self-discipline shows us Chaucer's difference from the Pardoner, but it also registers the power of the impulse and gives us the Pardoner himself in all his pride and despair, questioning and mocking in a voice of his own that disquiets us yet.

The Pardoner's Homosexuality and How It Matters

Monica E. McAlpine

The famous pronouncement of Chaucer's narrator on Chaucer's Pardoner—"I trowe he were a geldyng or a mare"—poses several questions for modern readers. What are the options that it offers for the interpretation of the Pardoner? Why is the narrator unable to decide between them? To what extent does Chaucer maintain this indeterminacy about the Pardoner and require the reader, like the narrator, to remain forever undecided? Does Chaucer in any way lead the reader to a greater certitude? If so, what is the sexual status of the Pardoner? Finally, what is the moral significance of that status? These questions arise partly from the complexity of Chaucer's poetry and partly from present-day ignorance of medieval sexual concepts and terminology.

The term "mare," in particular, has proved notoriously difficult for modern readers to interpret, and even when the term is glossed, the possibility that the Pardoner may be a "mare" is often ignored in favor of the belief that he is certainly a "geldyng," or eunuch. Psychological, moral, and spiritual interpretations of the Pardoner's eunuchry and of the sterility and, less accurately, the impotence with which it is associated permeate current critical treatments of this pilgrim. A faithful reading of Chaucer's line requires that the balance be restored. We need a gloss for "mare," and we need interpretations of the Pardoner's portrait and of his prologue and tale that explore

From *PMLA* 95, no. 1 (January 1980). © 1980 by the Modern Language Association of America.

the implications of his possible status as "mare" just as fully as criticism has already explored the implications of his possible status as "geldyng." It is neither likely nor desirable that such a reading will replace the view of the Pardoner as a eunuch; rather, it is to be hoped it will shed new light on familiar aspects of Chaucer's rich characterization.

As a contribution to this work, I wish to offer, in the first and longer part of this essay, a more detailed argument than has so far been attempted in favor of viewing the Pardoner as a possible homosexual. In the second part, I consider the spiritual implications of the Pardoner's sexuality by redirecting attention to his bagful of pardons and relics. The initial references to these objects occupy a significant place in the middle section of the Pardoner's tripartite portrait in the General Prologue: he is not only a "geldyng or a mare" (ll. 669–91) but also both a "pardoner" peddling false relics (ll. 692–706) and a "noble ecclesiaste" (ll. 704–14). Through an interpretation of the Pardoner as homosexual, I hope to confirm what this structure suggests: that his pardons and relics constitute the essential link, the lifeline, between this sexually anomalous Christian and his church.

I

For many of Chaucer's readers, the narrator's pronouncement is intimately linked with certain deservedly influential commentaries on the Pardoner's sexual status, and any reconsideration of the subject must acknowledge its debt to those studies and carefully discriminate its conclusions from theirs. In this ground-breaking review of medieval texts on medicine and physiognomy, Walter Clyde Curry opened discussion of the Pardoner's physical nature. Although the point is seldom noticed, Curry interprets the narrator's pronouncement as offering a choice between impotence and effeminacy. He treats the mention of these two sexual phenomena as serving to define a third possibility, underlying and unnamed, and then shows that the Pardoner's physical characteristics—long, fine hair; high voice; glaring eyes; and beardlessness—fit the descriptions of eunuchs offered by medieval doctors and physiognomists. All but one of Curry's sources, moreover, associate eunuchry with immorality, and some also insist that the congenital eunuch is more evil than the castrated eunuch. The sins attributed to eunuchs include dissoluteness, shamelessness, cunning, and viciousness. In what has proved the least convincing part of his argument, Curry contends that the other pilgrims, and Chaucer's audience, would have been able to go beyond the narrator's speculations to deduce that the Pardoner suffers from the (presumably rare) condition of congenital eunuchry.

Since in the view of the medieval experts the physical characteristics of all eunuchs are much the same, Curry's labeling of the Pardoner as a *congenital* eunuch is grounded not in unarguable physiognomical fact, as is sometimes believed, but in fallible literary interpretation. One argument appeals to the influence of source. Chaucer may have based his Pardoner, in part, on the characterization of a eunuch by the physiognomist Polemon, and Curry assumes that because Polemon's eunuch was a congenital eunuch, Chaucer's must be, too. A second argument rests on Curry's own estimate of the Pardoner's character; the depth of the Pardoner's depravity is seen as justifying his classification with the more malicious congenital eunuchs rather than with the comparatively benign castrated eunuchs. Moreover, by concentrating on the moral distinction between congenital eunuchs and castrated eunuchs, a prominent distinction in his sources, Curry distracts his readers from what he himself understands to be the different distinction in the General Prologue: that between "geldyng" and "mare." While he reveals the accuracy with which Chaucer uses the stereotype of the eunuch for some of the details of the Pardoner's portrait, Curry neither proves that the Pardoner is a congenital eunuch nor definitively exhausts the implications of the narrator's pronouncement.

The relationship of the Pardoner's eunuchry to his spiritual condition and to the larger themes of Chaucer's work was first addressed in a sophisticated way by Robert Miller. Miller examines medieval biblical glosses that attempt to resolve a conflict in attitudes toward eunuchs in the Old Testament. Deuteronomy 23:1, reflecting a literal-minded racial and sexual perception of holiness, excludes eunuchs from the temple, while Isaiah 56:3–5, taking a more spiritual approach, gives assurances that righteous eunuchs are among God's people. The medieval commentators found a solution to this conflict in a statement of Christ's discriminating among congenital eunuchs, involuntary castrates, and "eunuchs who have made themselves such for the Kingdom of heaven" (Matt. 19:12). Identifying the last group, the voluntary celibates in the service of God, as the eunuchs of Isaiah who will be accepted by God, the commentators go on to invent a second group of metaphorical eunuchs who will be rejected, as in Deuteronomy: those who, while capable of good works, deliberately remain spiritually sterile. Miller argues that the Pardoner's physical eunuchry is the sign of his deliberate spiritual sterility. His chosen role as *eunuchus non Dei* is seen as bitterly satiric, since he has a special responsibility as a churchman to be a *eunuchus Dei,* fruitful in good works.

If, however, Chaucer did use the Pardoner's physical condition as a sign in this way, he ran a considerable risk of undermining the very spiritual values he was attempting to communicate. Both Christ and the medieval commentators were reacting against the physical determinism of one strain of Jewish tradition. For them, involuntary eunuchry had no necessary moral significance at all; they were attempting to free the career of the soul from questions of genital competency. Miller's Pardoner, in contrast, is a static figure. While Miller rightly emphasizes the free action by which the Pardoner would have become a *eunuchus non Dei,* he does not recognize in Chaucer's characterization a continuing human potential for change. Because the immutable physical fact of eunuchry is taken as the sign of the Pardoner's spiritual status, his soul cannot be allowed its own career independent of his sexual destiny. Despite this difficulty, Miller's study has done more than any other to establish the level of seriousness on which the problem of the Pardoner's sexuality should be addressed. Moreover, the biblical materials he has brought to our attention can now be seen as documenting one kind of consideration that medieval people gave to a question central to Chaucer's characterization of the Pardoner: What is the place of sexually different, or "deviant," persons in the scheme of salvation?

Wide acceptance of the conclusions of Curry and Miller has had the unintended side effect of dulling reader's responses to the Pardoner; this pilgrim, it seems, has been fully "explained." As Donald Howard puts it in *The Idea of the* Canterbury Tales, the theory of the Pardoner's congenital and "scriptural" eunuchry has become an excuse for not taking him seriously. In his dazzling treatment of the Pardoner as a grotesque, as a "feminoid" or "hermaphroditic" male, Howard succeeds in re-creating the strangeness of this pilgrim—his power to mystify, frighten, and fascinate. Partly from motives of anger and revenge, the Pardoner alienates himself from the community of human and divine values; in

Howard's view, he becomes—like evil itself as defined in medieval philosophy, like the grotesques in manuscript illuminations, and like the very fragment of the *Canterbury Tales* in which his tale appears—something "on the periphery of the ordered world of created goodness," "marginal," "floating," "outside," "demonic." Curiously, Howard accepts as fact the congenital and "scriptural" eunuchry that theorists have attributed to the Pardoner and claims that we know the character's sexual status while the narrator and the others do not. His discussion of the Pardoner nevertheless proceeds, rightly I think, as if we share the same general perspective as the pilgrims—that is, as if we too remain uncertain about the Pardoner's sexual status and thus experience the whole man as mysterious.

Howard fears that any interpretation of the Pardoner as homosexual would "explain" the Pardoner in the same deadening and unprofitable way as the belief in the character's eunuchry has and that the modern stereotype of the effeminate male homosexual would be anachronistically used to deny the Pardoner's mystery. While I agree that the danger of another reductive reading is real, a view of the Pardoner as homosexual would not necessarily have this effect; for the danger lies not in any particular sexual definition but in the manner of relating the Pardoner's sexuality to his spirituality. Nor is the stereotype of effeminate male homosexuality an anachronism; it is as authentically medieval as it is modern. Indeed, the medieval confusion of homosexuality with effeminacy and, as we shall see, with other sexual phenomena indicates both that Chaucer's contemporaries tried to explain homosexuality to themselves and that they failed to dispel the mystery it presented to them. It is true, however, that I cannot produce a Pardoner quite so enigmatic as Howard's, but this difference arises not from our disagreement about the Pardoner's possible homosexuality but from my unwillingness to accept, with Howard, the Pardoner's definition of himself as a "ful vicious man." By turning our attention from the standard glosses on the Pardoner's sexuality to the literary characterization itself, Howard has brought the Pardoner alive again; but in his valuable explication of the Pardoner as a grotesque, he accepts too fully the Pardoner's own tortured and theatrical self-image. While giving detailed consideration to the possibility that the Pardoner is isolated from his heterosexual and homophobic peers by a condition of homosexuality, I emphasize the Pardoner's identity as a pilgrim in the fellowship of other pilgrims, motivated, even in his cupidity, by the love they all seek and experiencing an anguished self-division not unlike what others suffer.

The first step in a reconsideration of the Pardoner's sexuality must be the establishment of a gloss for "mare." "Geldyng" and "mare" are homely metaphors that must have had meanings both familiar and fairly precise for Chaucer's medieval audience; modern readers, however, face difficulties in recovering these meanings. Curry's influence is registered, but often inaccurately or incompletely, in modern editions of the *Canterbury Tales*. Among recent editors, only Donald R. Howard glosses both "geldyng" and "mare," and he interprets the first as "castrated eunuch" and the second as "congenital eunuch." John Hurt Fisher preserves Curry's too narrow interpretation of "geldyng" as suggesting impotence, while Albert Baugh reflects what I think is the most common understanding of Curry's argument (and of the Pardoner's status): that "geldyng" means "eunuch" (without implying any differentiation of types) and that the Pardoner is a eunuch. Neither Fisher nor Baugh, however, repeats Curry's interpretation of "mare" as a reference to effeminacy or offers any alternative gloss for that word. Finally, while both the *Middle English Dictionary* and the *Oxford English Dictionary* fully document the use of "geldyng" as a term for "eunuch," neither includes any evidence for a meaning of "mare" relevant to Chaucer's context.

For many modern readers, the obvious possible translations for "mare" are "effeminate male" and "homosexual male." Until recently, though, there appeared to be no evidence that the word had been used in either of these senses. Then, in 1973, Jill Mann pointed to a Latin poem by the twelfth-century satirist Walter of Chatillôn in which homosexual men, also described as effeminate, are labeled "mares": "equa fit equus" ("the horse becomes a mare"). While it is not certain that Chaucer knew Walter's works, they were relatively well known in England, and the poem does add weight to the suggestion that "mare" may mean "effeminate male" or "homosexual male" or both. But even if there were no question about Chaucer's having read the poem, one supporting text would not constitute proof of his meaning.

We need not wait for the discovery of more supporting texts, however. The details of the Pardoner's portrait and the term "geldyng" create a context that suggests criteria for glossing "mare." "Mare" must be a term commonly used in Chaucer's day to designate a male person who, though not necessarily sterile or impotent, exhibits physical traits suggestive of femaleness, visible characteristics that were also associated with eunuchry in medieval times and that were thought to have broad effects on the psyche and on character. The gloss that most satisfactorily fulfills these criteria is "a homosexual." Chaucer did not know the word "homosexual," of course, since it did not enter the language until 1869, but he might have referred to what we call homosexuality by making a biblical reference (to sodomites), a mythological reference (to Ganymede or Orpheus), a historical reference (to Julius Caesar, for example), or a philosophical reference (to sinners against nature). As we shall see, the choice of "mare" has several important and related advantages: it avoids provoking an immediate response of condemnation, which other references might have invited; it focuses attention not on sexual acts but on a type of person in whose soma and psyche Chaucer apparently believed homosexuality to be deeply rooted; and it suggests an attitude on the narrator's part in keeping with his character—a mixture of sympathy, amusement, and condescension.

Since several historical accounts are available, I shall not pause to document in detail the familiarity of Chaucer's audience with male homosexuality; I should like to explore instead the situation reflected in my criteria for glossing "mare," the confusion of homosexuality with other sexual phenomena.

In using a word denoting femaleness, Chaucer reflects one ancient and widespread misunderstanding about male homosexuality, that it involves a man's becoming in some sense a woman. The concept of effeminacy provides one way of thinking about this supposed transformation, but care must be taken in interpreting references to effeminacy in the medieval setting. The *Middle English Dictionary* records only two uses of the word "effeminate," both in the sense "self-indulgent" or "unreasonable." Satires on the fop, often described as long-haired and beardless, reflect a perception of feminization of behavior and appearance without any necessary suggestion of homosexuality. In medieval Latin, however, *effeminatus* sometimes means "homosexual," as in the Vulgate Bible, and this sense had passed into English by the time of the King James Bible. There is some evidence, moreover, that the young aristocrat who aspired to fashion had to be careful to observe the boundaries that marked off effeminacy and homosexuality. At the end of a lengthy set of instructions on conduct, dress, and grooming in

Guillaume de Lorris's *Roman de la rose,* for example, the God of Love
tells the young lover:

> Cous tes manches, tes cheveus pigne,
> Mais ne te farde ne ne guigne:
> Ce n'apartient s'as dames non,
> Ou a ceus de mauvais renon,
> Qui amors par male aventure
> Ont trovees contre Nature.
>
> (ll. 2169–74)

Sew your sleeves and comb your hair, but do not rouge or
paint your face, for such a custom belongs only to ladies or
to men of bad repute, who have had the misfortune to find
a love contrary to Nature.

(trans. Charles Dahlberg)

Just as not all effeminate males were suspected of homosexuality, so not all homosexual males were perceived as effeminate. In his
translation of Dante's *Inferno,* Mark Musa notes the contrast between
the effeminate speech patterns of the sodomitical clerks in canto 15
and the more robust manner of the sodomitical soldiers in canto 16.
Since the substance of what constitutes effeminacy in males is
culturally defined and subject to change, it is not necessary to find in
the Middle Ages exact replicas of our current stereotype of effeminacy in homosexual males (including, for example, distinctive walk
or hand movements); it is only necessary to show that certain types
of feminized behavior and appearance in males were sometimes
interpreted as evidence of homosexuality. Thus, even if the primary
meaning of "mare" was "an effeminate male," a second meaning
may have been "a possibly homosexual male."

Another ancient way of conceiving the male homosexual's
supposed participation in the feminine was to think of him as a
hermaphrodite. In Hellenic rites and legends, the hermaphrodite is a
double god, a being with the overt equipment of both sexes (i.e.,
male genitals and female breasts), a symbol of unity, fruitfulness, and
eternal life. In Hellenistic art, however, the hermaphrodite is an
extremely feminized creature, though recognizably male, representative of one ideal of homosexual beauty. Interest in this type of
hermaphrodite revived during the twelfth-century resurgence of
classical scholarship. A late and perhaps unconscious reflection of this
tradition, evidence of its thorough absorption into European think-

ing, appears in the treatment of the story of Sodom and Gomorrah in the Middle English *Purity*, a work commonly ascribed to the *Gawain* poet. The poet describes Lot's first glimpse of the angels as they pass through the crowded streets of Sodom toward his house; they are extraordinarily beautiful young men with beardless chins, rosy complexions, and luxurious hair like raw silk:

> As he stared into þe strete þer stout men played,
> He syʒe þer swey in asent swete men tweyne;
> Bold burnez were þay boþe, wyth berdles chynnez,
> Royl rollande fax, to raw sylk lyke,
> Of ble as þe brere-flor where so þe bare schew[e]d;
> Ful clene watz þe countenaunce of her cler yʒen;
> Wlonk whit watz her wede and wel hit hem sem[e]d.
>
> (ll. 787–93)

On one level the beauty of the angels is meant to suggest a spiritual excellence superior to all considerations and distinctions of human sexuality; but as A. C. Spearing remarks, it also explains something left unexplained in the biblical text: how the men of Sodom came to desire homosexual intercourse with the angels. It seems likely that a hermaphroditic or feminoid male would have been suspected of sexual deviance.

An alternative to thinking of the male homosexual as a woman-man was to think of him as a nonman, for homosexuality was long confused with eunuchry. In Gautier de Leu's thirteenth-century fabliau "La Veuve," for example, a widow who remarries finds the vigorous sexual performance of her new husband on the wedding night nonetheless disappointing:

> Nos avons çaiens un bruhier,
> un durfeüt, un hebohet.
> Ahi! con Damerdex me het
> qui fui des bons vallés aquius,
> et des cortois et des gentius,
> si pris cest caitif par nature.
>
> . . . .
>
> Et cis ribaus me tient plus vil
> que le femier de son cortil,
> mais je sai bien, par Saint Eloi,
> qu'il n'est mie de bone loi,

ains est de çaus del Mont Wimer:
il n'a soing de dames amer.

What have we here? An impotent,
beardless ne'er-do-well! Ah me!
The Lord must hate me bitterly,
who turned away from fine young men,
well born, courteous, and then
wound up with this congenital bum!

. . . .

This scoundrel shows me less regard
than he does the dungheap in the yard.
However, by Saint Loy I know
his moral code is just as low
as that of those on Mount Wimer;
for woman's love he doesn't care.

(trans. Robert Harrison)

The widow equates less than heroic sexual performance with impotence, impotence with beardless eunuchry, both of these with homosexuality, and all of these with heresy, for the reference to Mount Wimer concerns a large group of *bougres* who were burned to death for homosexuality and heresy in Champagne in 1239. The fabliau makes fun of the widow and her insatiable appetite, but the intended comedy of her speech must have depended partly on the pervasiveness of just such misunderstandings; at the same time, the poet who made comedy out of the widow's confusion must himself have been in some degree superior to it. Like the French poet, Chaucer may be seen as making artistic use of what he perceived to be a common misunderstanding of sexual phenomena. The Pardoner's possible eunuchry may contribute to the portrait of a homosexual since medieval people apparently strove to understand homosexuality by identifying it with now one, now another, sexual anomaly.

Seen against this background, Chaucer's portrait of the Pardoner in the General Prologue emerges as a pastiche of allusions to the three distinct sexual phenomena with which homosexuality was often confused—effeminacy, hermaphroditism, and eunuchry—and thus very probably to homosexuality itself. In the order of their appearance in the portrait the allusions are the description of the Pardoner's hair—its length and fineness suggesting effeminacy, eunuchry, and hermaphroditism and his grooming of it suggesting effeminacy; the Pardoner's concern with fashion, implying effeminacy; the references to goats and hares, suggesting hermaphroditism; the high voice, connoting effeminacy and eunuchry; the glaring eyes, associated with eunuchry; and the beardlessness, a symptom of effeminacy, eunuchry, hermaphroditism, and homosexuality. Furthermore, the glaring eyes and the references to goats, hares, and mares connote extreme lechery, which is at least as suggestive of sexual deviance as of sexual inadequacy. What this catalog shows is that most of the allusions tend to be *multivalent,* and the reason is that the lines between these various sexual phenomena were fluid in medieval theory. It is impossible to say whether beardlessness, for example, was more likely to suggest eunuchry or homosexuality to a medieval person. Because of this fluidity, too, references to effeminacy, hermaphroditism, and eunuchry could serve as a code for homosexuality. Finally, while the categories "effeminate," "hermaphrodite," and "eunuch" can each account for some of the Pardoner's characteristics, only the category "homosexual" can account for all of them. For example, while the Pardoner's interest in fashion can be referred directly only to effeminacy (and not to eunuchry or hermaphroditism) and the narrator's allusion to goats only to hermaphroditism, both can be referred to homosexuality through what the medieval audience regarded as the mediating concepts of effeminacy and hermaphroditism.

Thus at a minimum it seems impossible to exclude the suggestion of homosexuality from the portrait. It is also impossible for the reader not to be influenced by the opening frame for this physical description: the presentation of the Pardoner's association with the Summoner. The nature of this association has long been debated, but there is no doubt that the Pardoner is introduced to us traveling with a male "friend" and "compeer" and that the two are singing, in their contrasting voices, a love song, "Com hider, love, to me" (ll. 670–71). This tableau may be read in two ways. The Pardoner may be seen as a frustrated heterosexual who associates himself with the lecherous Summoner in order to deny his own impotence and to acquire symbolically the Summoner's virility; or he may be seen as a homosexual, ambivalent about disclosing his status, who nonetheless becomes suspect through the public display of this ambiguous friendship. These are the two possibilities that the narrator makes explicit, I believe, when he provides the closing frame for the physical description of the Pardoner: "I trowe he were a geldyng or a mare." Thus these three parts of the Pardoner's portrait—the opening tableau, the physical description, and the closing pronouncement—fit together in a way that has not been fully appreciated. For the medieval audience, with its confused and limited lexicon of sexual terms and concepts, it was the physical description, I suspect, that was most ambiguous; the opening frame first provided implicit guidance, and the closing frame then explicit guidance, to its interpretation. Modern readers may have a different experience, since the meaning of the Pardoner's friendship with the Summoner has been clouded by controversy and the meaning of the term "mare" has long been lost. In this situation, the physical description, once it is set in the context of medieval sexual theory, seems to me to provide the strongest evidence of the Pardoner's possible homosexuality, which in turn helps us both to recognize a possible implication of his association with the Summoner and to gloss "mare."

Given, then, that Chaucer's text explicitly and implicitly raises the issue of homosexuality, the narrator's treatment of the Pardoner seems to unfold in this way. Faced with a somewhat bewildering set of indications to interpret, the narrator rather shrewdly cuts through the complexity to suggest that the Pardoner is either a nonman, that is, a eunuch, or a woman-man, a homosexual. Indeed the phrase "I trowe," which may denote either speculation or certainty, serves to dramatize the narrator in his role as interpreter, dealing confidently yet respectfully with resistant reality. There may even be an element of self-congratulation in his announced inability to decide exactly what the Pardoner's status is; the narrator may think that the double reference to eunuchry and homosexuality displays his sophistication. Actually, though, he is rather like the modern person who has not mastered the distinctions among homosexuals, bisexuals, transvestites, and transsexuals. One consequence of the narrator's characteristically limited perception is that we initially encounter the Pardoner as a kind of puzzle to be solved rather than as a pilgrim to be judged.

The animal imagery of the narrator's pronouncement also helps temporarily to isolate the Pardoner from moral judgment. The narrator perceives the Pardoner as someone conspicuously deficient in the animal sphere of perfection, lacking integrity of sexual identity, physical intactness, or procreative competency—the amoral perfections, elaborated in various cultural forms, that the narrator admires in the Monk and Harry Bailey. Though found wanting in one sphere, the Pardoner is perceived as supremely competent in another; thus the significance of the "but" as the narrator turns to the Pardoner's work in the world: "But of his craft, fro Berwyk into Ware, / Ne was ther swich another pardoner" (ll. 692–93). Sheer expertise, unrelated to its use or purpose, is one of the narrator's chief measures of value throughout the General Prologue, and this ideal, despite its moral limitations, has a special virtue in regard to the Pardoner since it embraces more than sexuality. For the narrator, the "pardoner" and the "noble ecclesiaste" are as important as the "geldyng" or the "mare." The narrator sets an example of not reducing the Pardoner to his sexuality, an example that at other levels of response Chaucer means us to emulate.

Nevertheless we cannot be so content with the narrator's tentative diagnosis of the Pardoner as the narrator himself is. As viewed by the medieval church, eunuchry and homosexuality had very different moral statuses; pace the doctors and physiognomists, eunuchry was not in itself regarded as sinful, while homosexual acts (the concept of a homosexual condition was not recognized by the moral theologians) were considered grave sins. From this standpoint the narrator's self-satisfied conclusion that the Pardoner is one thing or the other is quite astonishing, for it reflects an essentially secular perspective. Since, however, we must view the Pardoner as a pilgrim—that is, not only as an animal being and an expert worker but also as a moral being with a spiritual destiny—we need to know more than the narrator is able to tell us. The narrator's comment on the Pardoner's sexual status preserves immutably for all time the narrator's own uncertainty about his fellow pilgrim. It does not fix to the same degree the mystery about the Pardoner himself, although the absence of any other explicit statement about his sexuality means that a choice between "geldyng" and "mare" or any extrapolation using both terms will always be an *interpretation*. Many critics, having chosen "geldyng," have traced the implications of their choice in readings of the Pardoner's prologue and tale; while admitting that the Pardoner may be a eunuch as well, I choose to emphasize his possible status as a "mare," or homosexual, and I should like to explore some of the consequences of my choice.

II

It is rather widely agreed that the avarice the Pardoner boasts about is a screen sin, concealing some graver defect of body or soul or both. Like his interpreters, the Pardoner betrays an interest in degrees of sinfulness, identifying one of the rioters in his tale as the "proudeste" (l. 716), another rioter (or perhaps the same one) as the "worste of hem" (l. 776), Harry Bailey as "moost envoluped in synne" (l. 942), and himself as "a ful vicious man" (l. 459). Also, as his constant preaching text, "*Radix malorum*" (l. 334), reveals, he is obsessively interested in underlying states of sinfulness, and other evidence suggests that he finds the root of all evil in the body. Although his semihysterical discussion of the so-called tavern sins seems not to rest on any positive values, it does have a unifying theme. All the sins are developed to some degree in a way that relates them to the human body.

Gluttony, of course, has a natural relation to the body, but the Pardoner's tracing of ingested food from "the tendre mouth" to the "shorte throte" (compared to a privy) to the "stynkyng cod, / Fulfilled of dong and of corrupcioun" and at last to the bowels with their "foul . . . soun" (ll. 512–35) tends to turn all eating into an obscene act. He even treats the sin of Adam and Eve as an act of gluttony, ignoring its intellectual content. Similarly, cursing is treated not as a rejection of Christ's divinity and teachings but as an attack on Christ's body; all the examples the Pardoner provides refer to Christ's body and passion, and he later says of the rioters "Cristes blessed body [they] torente" (l. 709). Finally, gambling is most dramatically presented to us in an imagined scene in which the dice are referred to as "bones" (l. 656). The treatment of these vices suggests an obsessive concern with the body as the source of sin, the instrument of sin, and the victim of sin. Significantly, avarice, the screen sin, is not presented as having an intimate connection with the body; instead it is decidedly intellectual, requiring of the Pardoner great cleverness in plying the tricks of his trade.

A key passage in the Pardoner's prologue hints more directly at what the concealed and deadly sinfulness in the body might be. The Pardoner describes one of his most ingenious tricks for persuading people to venerate his relics and offer alms:

> Goode men and wommen, o thyng warne I yow:
> If any wight be in this chirche now
> That hath doon synne horrible, that he
> Dar nat, for shame, or it yshryven be,
> Or any womman, be she yong or old,

> That hath ymaad hir housbonde cokewold,
> Swich folk shal have no power ne no grace
> To offren to my relikes in this place.
>
> (ll. 377–84)

The specificity about the woman's sin and the lack of specificity about the man's provoke interpretation. It seems likely that the unnamed sin shares a number of characteristics with infidelity: it is a sexual sin; it is peculiarly associated with one sex—with men, as culpable infidelity had long been associated with women; and it inspires a special opprobrium that arises from a cultural bias rather than from the principles of Christian ethics. Male homosexuality meets all these criteria. Most important, the shame that attends the naming of the sin even in the confessional seems a clear allusion to homosexuality. Long before homosexuality was christened by Lord Alfred Douglas "the Love that dare not speak its name," it had been commonly referred to in some variation of the formula found in Chaucer's Parson's Tale: "thilke abhomynable synne, of which that no man unnethe oghte speke ne write."

It would be wrong to seem to deny, by qualification, the intense homophobia embodied in this notorious phrase, and yet it is important to recognize that there were shadings of opinion and feeling about homosexuality. In the *Canterbury Tales* the Pardoner's behavior and the reactions of the other pilgrims reflect a setting in which a homosexual person, while possibly aware of the severe penalties sometimes inflicted on his kind, did not feel a proximate fear for his safety. The Pardoner's flaunting of his friendship with the Summoner, though undoubtedly compulsive behavior, is probably not undertaken without some realistic assessment of the risks. As the pilgrims' apprehension about his ribaldry and Harry's false camaraderie suggest, what the Pardoner must confront in others is not their outright condemnation of him but their discomfiture, with its varying degrees of amusement, fear, sympathy, disgust, and ambiguous tolerance. In ministers of the church's sacraments, like Chaucer's Parson, the Pardoner would almost certainly encounter at least unthinking, if not vehement, reflections of that homophobia which the church had helped both to create and to perpetuate. In himself, the Pardoner has to contend with that self-hatred which internalizes the judgments of others. Ultimately the man who cannot confess the unnamed and unnameable sin is the Pardoner himself.

It may well be, moreover, that the Pardoner's inability to approach the confessional arises partly from his perception of the gulf between what the church was prepared to forgive and what he had to confess. As his portrait suggests, the Pardoner's homosexuality is a profound part of his being, an aspect that Chaucer could portray (and probably conceive of) only by projecting a biological cause. The Pardoner himself seems to feel that he is in a state of alienation from Christ and the church, a state that is more than the sum of his sinful acts. *Mala,* or specific evil deeds, are not his concern; the *radix,* or root condition, is. But in the matter of homosexuality, as in matters of human sexuality generally, the church's moral theology tended to focus on acts, not on persons; and while it took account of a variety of actors, it defined them in terms of certain fixed statuses only: young or old, male or female, married or unmarried, clerical or lay. It understood homosexual acts only as the perverse behavior of basically heterosexual persons. In other words, the church was prepared to deal with sinners like the scabby Summoner but not with the tortured Pardoner. The "inverted" Pardoner did not fit the church's definitions and could scarcely form a sincere purpose to amend a condition in himself he probably felt he had no power to change. Chaucer's study of homosexuality in the Pardoner seems to represent a deliberate intention to explore the inner reality of an outcast especially despised by his society and especially misunderstood by his church.

It is no accident that the man who cannot confess becomes a pardoner. Seizing on a theologically marginal church practice, the granting of indulgences, the Pardoner subverts the sacrament of penance he cannot use while simultaneously setting himself up as a substitute confessor. Officially, he had the power to offer almsgivers only remission of the punishment due sins already absolved by a priest. In practice, like many actual pardoners, he sold supposed absolution from sin. While some of his customers may have been naive Christians who could not appreciate the difference, others must have hoped to buy spiritual safety dishonestly, without reforming their lives. By exploiting the potential for self-deceit in those he imagines condemn him, the Pardoner attempts to convict his customers of being themselves "envoluped in synne." As he leads them away from the legitimate sacrament, it is as if he were saying, "If I cannot be truly forgiven, neither shall they be." At the same time, the Pardoner constantly enacts in reverse the scene of absolution he longs for. As he dispenses his own brand of absolution, often arousing in his audience true contrition (ll. 430–31), it is as if he were saying, "If there is anyone the church will not forgive, I will forgive him," all the while hoping that the forgiveness he dispenses will magically flow back to cleanse himself.

This manipulation of the sacrament is one of the things the Pardoner does that tend to be obscured by what he says as he constructs a smoke screen of single-minded avarice. But his intimate association with confession betrays, beneath his practiced cynicism, the seriousness with which he regards the sacrament. Apparently he does not allow himself the easy out he offers others—the chance to buy forgiveness and satisfaction with money or specific good works. For himself the Pardoner requires true contrition, true purpose of amendment: he *does* believe that Christ's pardon is best.

Interestingly, it was the subversion of the sacrament, more than the misappropriation of funds, that other churchmen principally complained of in actual pardoners. But Chaucer's association of his Pardoner with false relics may be a more imaginative touch, since it is not especially characteristic of the pardoners described in contemporary documents. Perhaps nothing else about the Pardoner expresses so poignantly his anguish about his body as do the jars and bottles of old bones and bits of clothing he always carries with him. When Harry Bailey charges that the Pardoner would try to pass off his "olde breech" "with [his] fundement depeint" as a relic and proposes to enshrine the Pardoner's testicles in a hog's turd "in stide of relikes or of seintuarie" (ll. 948–55), the symbolic equivalence between the relics and the Pardoner himself becomes almost explicit. For many readers, Harry's crudity must suddenly and explosively bring to consciousness a truth they have already apprehended subliminally.

Binding himself again to a marginal expression of the church's life, the veneration of relics, the Pardoner expresses both his fear, nearing conviction, that his own body, like the tavern in his tale, is the devil's temple (l. 470) and his faint but continuing hope that this same body may yet prove to be the holy temple of God. Because he uses false relics to make money and to entice others away from true contrition, the relics become, like his body, sources of sin to himself and to others. Moreover, by offering the relics for veneration, he dupes his customers into kissing what is symbolically his instrument of that sodomitical sin he and they have learned to despise. At the same time, the Pardoner seems always to be hoping that others will repose a genuine faith in his relics, a faith that will miraculously transform his relics and the body they represent into holy things. In all his traffickings with relics, the plea for money is partly a camouflage for the plea for the redemptive kiss. The relics he uses for this purpose *must* be false. His relics must be as unholy as he thinks his body is so that the hoped-for transformation can be "real." The Pardoner will never experience such a transformation, of course, since he will never be able to respect the faith of those he deceives and corrupts.

The notorious difficulty of accounting for the Pardoner's offering to the pilgrims relics he has already admitted to be false arises in part from overemphasizing the mercenary motive. But by taking the pilgrims into his confidence to a degree, the Pardoner has developed a more intimate relationship with his audience than he usually develops with his more gullible victims. In offering relics now, he is acting under an unusually strong compulsion to acquire that personal validation he is always seeking through them. Even on this occasion, though, the Pardoner's attempt to reach out to Harry Bailey and the community he represents is doomed by the inveterate ambivalence of the Pardoner's own attitudes.

The latent aggression in the Pardoner's statement that Harry "shalt kisse the relikes everychon" (l. 944) and the latent sexual implication in his command to Harry to "Unbokele anon thy purs" (l. 945) turn the scene into one of implied seduction or even rape; the Pardoner uses his homosexuality as a weapon. In addition, by characterizing Harry as "envoluped in synne" (l. 942) and offering to pardon Harry's sins, the Pardoner contemptuously portrays the heterosexual Christian as needing the absolution of the despised sodomite. But with the same gesture with which he assaults Harry's heterosexual sensitivities, the Pardoner asks for love; and with the same gesture with which he charges another with sin, he seeks forgiveness for himself. Understandably Harry reacts to the threats to himself in the Pardoner's behavior and does not hear the cry for acceptance. Example of natural manhood that he is, Harry retaliates by casting aspersions on the Pardoner's virility and by threatening castration (ll. 946–55). But as the reference to the true relic of Saint Helen's cross suggests, the ultimate issue is not perfection in the physical order but holiness in the spiritual order. The Pardoner's defeat lies in the clear implication of Harry's obscenity that both the Pardoner's relics and his body are *not holy*.

The goal of the final scene, as of all the Pardoner's maneuvers, is a kiss. The scene does in fact end with a kiss, of course, though not one of the sort the Pardoner was seeking. The Knight engineers a reconciliation between Harry and the Pardoner that restores a degree of mutual tolerance while avoiding all the issues. We may be thankful, though, that the Pardoner does not receive the kiss that in rage and self-contempt he wished to extort from an abased Harry. It would truly have been an obscene kiss, not because of any homo-sexual element, but because of its sadomasochistic nature. Left unanswered, however, is the question whether the Pardoner will ever receive the kiss that in another sense he was seeking: not a kiss mirroring his own self-contempt or a kiss of ambivalent social tolerance but a kiss expressing genuine acceptance of his humanity— in Christian terms, a kiss confirming his part in the Father's creation and in the Son's redemption.

Through his manipulation of the sacrament of penance, the Pardoner covertly seeks forgiveness for what he takes to be his sinful condition; through his manipulation of relics, he covertly seeks affirmation that he is in some sense holy. The Pardoner lives his life through the church's rituals, sacraments, and sacramentals in a way that dramatizes both the pain of exclusion and the hope for ultimate inclusion. No other pilgrim is so saturated in the life of the institutional church as this accomplished singer of the liturgy, this eloquent preacher steeped in the lore of the pulpit, and this successful entrepreneur in absolutions and relics. Though believing himself the church's rejected son, the Pardoner has done everything he can to make himself a "noble ecclesiaste."

Given the position of the medieval church on homosexuality, this interpretation of the Pardoner might seem to offer new grounds for the still current belief that the Pardoner is, among Chaucer's pilgrims, uniquely evil. In my view it does no such thing. Ideally this interpretation should help us to penetrate the Pardoner's own obfuscatory characterization of himself as "a ful vicious man," a characterization that has already begun to receive the skeptical criticism it deserves. Making a useful distinction between behavior and state of mind, John Halverson shows that the Pardoner probably does less actual harm than the Friar and that his description of his own spiritual condition is preposterous, serving to mock those who accept it while disguising and protecting the Pardoner's true self. Halverson finds the Pardoner not evil, but deadly, "necrophiliac." While the relationship of the Pardoner to death is important and deserves the further study Halverson calls for, I think it is already possible to say that the Pardoner's manipulation of relics and pardons betrays signs of spiritual life.

Interestingly, the subject of homosexuality offers Chaucer the opportunity to distinguish between behavior and state of mind in much the same way as Halverson does. Any physical acts in which the Pardoner expressed his homosexuality would be viewed by the medieval church as sinful, and Chaucer does not challenge this teaching. But he does challenge the belief that such sins are uniquely abhorrent, poisoning the whole character and extirpating all good and all potential for good. The Pardoner's elaborate way of relating to church and community through his relics and pardons reveals such hopeful signs as a latent belief in his own essential worthiness, a desire to be restored to God's grace, a desire to be socially useful, and a desire to give and receive love. The Pardoner's defenses, even against the best in himself, are so well entrenched, however, that the possibility of a transformation seems remote, though it cannot be denied. The Pardoner's preaching text, "*Radix malorum est Cupiditas*," is only one of the mottoes relevant to the judgment of this pilgrim; the other is the snatch of popular song on his lips when we first meet him, "Com hider, love, to me." It is sometimes said that this song refers only to carnal love, and to a love made distasteful by the characters of the Summoner and the Pardoner. But just as Chaucer alludes here to that charity which is the cardinal value of his pilgrimage, so the Pardoner, however unconsciously, names this charity as the ultimate goal of his own yearnings. Cupidity and love—each reader must decide what relative weight to give to these two in judging the Pardoner, and the weighting of the balances is not obvious.

The task of judging the Pardoner, like that of judging each of the other pilgrims, makes the judges vulnerable, too, not least of all Chaucer himself. A final question cannot be evaded. Why does Chaucer treat the possibility of the Pardoner's homosexuality so allusively? Does his indirection betray some allegiance, or at least some submission, to the phobic view that homosexuality is so abhorrent it must not be spoken or written about? We must admit, on the one hand, that here Chaucer may be showing a characteristic degree of caution. On the other hand, Chaucer's very silences can be seen as an allusion to the sin that should not be named. Such an argument runs the risk of being merely self-serving for the critic, of course; but if the glossing of "mare" as "homosexual" is accepted, then the interpretation of Chaucer's other allusions has a firm anchor in the literal meaning of the text. Moreover, what I take to be this explicit suggestion of possible homosexuality is never withdrawn or disproved. Thus readers must engage in a work of interpretation that inescapably becomes a moral exercise. Because the facts about the Pardoner's sexuality are not given but must be established, readers cannot easily retreat into one-dimensional judgments of this pilgrim; they are forced to consider the whole character of the Pardoner in a way that should in turn contribute to a nonreductive appreciation of his sexuality and its spiritual implications.

Chaucer may have been inspired by a conviction like the one with which the Parson closes his discussion of "thilke abhomynable synne": "though that hooly writ speke of horrible synne, certes hooly writ may not been defouled, namoore than the sonne that shyneth on the mixne." Chaucer may be seen as using his art, and especially its indirection and allusiveness, to challenge the sexual phobias of his readers, requiring them mentally to juxtapose the Pardoner's countenance with Christ's, even as the Pardoner himself has done by wearing a vernicle on his cap. The vernicle, a representation of Christ's face as it appeared on Veronica's veil, was commonly worn by Christians who had made pilgrimage to Rome. There is nothing unusual about the Pardoner's wearing such an emblem (although another pilgrim to Rome, the Wife of Bath, is apparently not wearing one), but Chaucer's use of it is nonetheless thematically significant. The vernicle asserts the dignity of the Pardoner, whatever his sexual status, as part of Christ and reminds us that through his sexual sufferings the Pardoner participates in the crucifixion. But most important, the vernicle asserts the necessity of each reader's responding to the Pardoner in the context of Christian love, a necessity that cannot be evaded by appeals to the values of secular society or to the prescriptions of ecclesiastical leaders. The use of the vernicle is daring, the challenge to the reader risky; Chaucer is not always cautious.

It would be wrong to overstate the special relation of the vernicle to the Pardoner, however, and thus to isolate him once again in his supposed uniqueness. The vernicle might be mentally placed on the headdresses of all the pilgrims; there is not one of them who does not challenge the observer's capacity for insight and love. The Pardoner will not be rightly judged until we also subject to judgment our own fascination with him and until we perceive what he shares with the other pilgrims as clearly as we perceive what sets him apart. Chaucer, after all, suggests the balance at the very beginning; he gives us a "compaignye, / Of sondry folk" but "pilgrimes were they alle."

Sermon Structure in the Pardoner's Tale

Robert P. Merrix

The relationship of the Pardoner's Prologue and Tale to the medieval sermon persists as a critical topic in contemporary Chaucerian scholarship. Opinion ranges from unequivocal acceptance of a specific relationship to unequivocal rejection. For Coolidge O. Chapman the tale was "a typical medieval sermon." For Susan Gallick, it is "more a bad joke than a sermon." Those who argue for a relationship are, in turn, divided when it comes to defining the nature of that relationship. Some (like F. N. Robinson) relate the poem to the sermon structurally; others (like Charles Shain) define the relationship "rhetorically." And Siegfried Wenzel, denying that the connection is either structural or rhetorical, asserts that Chaucer merely borrowed "technical terms, specific images, and story plots" from "contemporary sermon literature" for all the *Canterbury Tales.*

The major problem in defining the relation of the tale to the medieval sermon arises from the assumption that the sermon was made up of clearly delineated parts within a unique structure. From this it follows that since this ideal, hypothetical sermon form cannot be superimposed on the Pardoner's Tale, the tale must not be a sermon. The second problem, stemming from the first, arises from the assumption that each part of a medieval sermon had a specific homiletic function. And since the parts of the Pardoner's Tale do not correspond to those functions, again it follows that the tale cannot be

From *The Chaucer Review* 17, no. 3 (1983). © 1983 by the Pennsylvania State University.

a sermon. These assumptions need to be tested, however, by an examination of the *artes praedicandi,* which supposedly codified the rules for sermon structure, and by an analysis of some representative medieval sermons, the so-called "modern" sermons which were the products of such theories. Such an analysis will show that these "modern" medieval sermons, though structurally more complex than the earlier, more casual sermons of Boniface and Peter Damian, are not so structurally rigid as we have been led to believe. A further analysis of the Pardoner's Tale in relation to the *artes praedicandi* and the sermons modeled on them will reveal similarities strong enough to term Chaucer's tale, structurally, a "modern" medieval sermon.

I

The principles of sermon-making grew out of the *artes praedicandi,* the medieval treatises on preaching compiled by the university clerics or teachers for the purpose of guiding prospective preachers in their art. The *artes praedicandi,* written by such men as Robert of Basevorn (*Forma Praedicandi*), Thomas Waleys (*De Modo Componendi Sermones*), and John of Wales among others, contain elaborate rules for the construction of sermons, in addition to practical advice on methods of sermon delivery. These treatises reflect the rise of the medieval universities and the growing influence of the teaching friars in the thirteenth and fourteenth centuries. Père Charland defines the new method thus:

> This "art of preaching," taught by masters distributed over a period from the thirteenth to the fifteenth centuries, presents itself, in the first place, as *modern.* It is modern, first of all, in regard to the eloquence of the Church Fathers, who, quickened by the Spirit, do not have to be confined within the narrow precepts of a man-made method, within a "forma praedicandi," as Robert Basevorn said. But it is modern also in a stricter sense, one recognized by our pedagogues: preaching has evolved. . . . No longer does one preach "the full gospel," as a type of sermon.
>
> (*Artes Praedicandi*)

Eventually the "plein évangile" came to be called the "ancient" as distinguished from the university or "modern" method of preaching, and the mode of distinction lay in an adherence to the formal rules. Although those rules were far from being standardized, an eclectic sampling of Basevorn, Waleys, and John of Wales furnishes certain elements that sermons were supposed to contain as severally argued. Briefly those elements were: (1) theme, (2) protheme, (3) the introduction to the theme, (4) the division of the theme, (5) the subdivision, and (6) the discussion. According to the treatise writers, these elements were to be developed systematically so that each element would rise naturally out of the preceding one.

Ideally, if these were the criteria of sermon-making during the later Middle Ages, one would expect to find among a representative group of medieval sermons some, if not all, faithfully conforming to the rules. Such, however, is not the case. In a group of fifty-one sermons edited by W. O. Ross, twenty-nine of which are classed as "modern," not one completely follows the theoretical pattern. Moreover, as Ross himself points out, the distinction between types is much less clear than one might expect. After suggesting that the sermons could be divided "roughly" into "the 'ancient' and the 'modern,' " he adds in a note:

> The word "roughly" in this sentence should be empha-
> sized. . . . All that can be said is that "modern" sermons
> tended to have certain features in common which sermons
> not belonging to this class did not possess.
>
> (*Middle English Sermons*)

The main point here is that Shain, Wenzel, and others use these "modern" sermons to argue a lack of formal structure or homiletic function in the Pardoner's Tale. Of the two sermons used by Shain, one (no. 39) has no introduction to the theme, and the other (no. 40) has neither protheme nor introduction, and, in fact, is not regarded by Ross as a "definite university type," but only one which shows "the influence of the 'modern' organization."

What then is the "systematic sermon structure" so freely appealed to by critics, and where may one find it? According to Charland, it lies in the treatises themselves. Speaking of the two principle treatises which developed the rhetorical rules of the modern sermon—those of Robert of Basevorn and Thomas Waleys—he says:

> These two treatises, like almost all those of the same type,
> are principally concerned with the learned sermon, to be
> pronounced before the University; it is only incidentally
> that they refer to the sermon which is to be made to the
> public.

The "systematic sermon structure," then, is a model that candidates for the Master of Theology degree followed in their *sermo examinatorius* at Oxford. Such sermons would naturally be composed in Latin and directed to a select and sophisticated audience of clerics. Consequently, the formal sermon is restricted to a specific location and audience.

Although the range of the sermon is limited, we would still expect to find within that area an adherence to and a basic agreement on the fundamental rules of the treatises. But again such is not the case. As Ross states, later preachers seemed to be losing sight of various elements of the structure and especially the original function of the protheme, which John of Wales insisted was for the specific purpose of introducing a prayer. Ross quotes a manuscript falsely assigned to a "Henry of Hesse" which states: "Prothema est prelocutio facta pro approbatione terminorum predicabilium in themate positorum." Moreover, in a late medieval treatise edited by Harry Caplan, the teacher speaks of the protheme as being "made for the proof of the terms of preaching present in the theme, through authoritative passages of the Bible and learned men." Again, we discover that Thomas Waleys did "not wholly approve of the use of an introduction," and Robert of Basevorn says that some preachers may offer a prayer immediately after uttering the theme and may or may not give another prayer at the end of the protheme.

The treatises themselves exhibit similar qualifications about whatever sermon pattern was chosen. Charles Smyth, following Robert of Basevorn and Thomas Waleys, says the rule by which a preacher must stick to his text (theme) "is not so rigid as to exclude the possibility of any extempore digression whatsoever, since the exigencies of human rhetoric must yield to the benefit of souls which is the end of preaching." We even note that Robert of Basevorn, the most "systematic" of the treatise writers, was not as inflexible as we are led to believe. In his *Forma Praedicandi* he speaks of the "distinctly modern sermon," but he restricts his concern to the "more famous" types of his "modern time" ("magis famoso secundum moderna tempora"). As Ross emphasizes, Basevorn's conflicting statements are warnings against believing that all medieval sermons of the "modern" type had precisely the same form.

These variations in the function of the sermon parts as voiced in the treatises and reflected in the sermons are echoed in attempts to formulate a common structural scheme. If such a common structure existed, scholars cannot agree on the nomenclature or the position of the elements themselves. Besides Ross's eclectic pattern already quoted, one finds these divergencies:

Charland	Chapman	Robinson	Owen
(1) theme	(1) theme	(1) theme	(1) theme
(2) protheme	(2) protheme	(2) protheme	(2) protheme
(3) introduction to theme	(3) division	(3) dilation	(3) restatement
(4) division	(4) subdivision	(4) exemplum	(4) introduction of theme
(5) confirmation of parts		(5) application	(5) process and development of principles
(6) development		(6) closing formula	(6) major exemplum

It is evident that only the position of the theme and protheme is agreed upon, and that both the terminology and position of the other elements vary and certainly are not indicative of a fixed or "systematic structure."

Here we must conclude, first, that if the "relation of the parts to the whole is the essence of medieval sermon-making," as Shain insists, then a model medieval sermon may not exist; and, second, that if each element of the medieval sermon must evince a specific function, a "systematic sermon structure" may not be found. A perfect medieval sermon, just as *a* perfect First Folio of Shakespeare, does not exist except as an abstraction. Thus to deny that the Pardoner's Tale is a medieval sermon because it does not follow the rules prescribed by the *artes praedicandi* writers is fallacious.

Consequently, we must modify the definition of the formal medieval sermon. It has neither a unique form nor function. Nevertheless, certain related elements exist in the "modern" medieval sermon which justify its being considered a valid genre. It differs considerably from the "ancient" sermon, sometimes partly in structure and sometimes in theme and style. A cursory examination of a collection of "older, freer forms," edited by J. M. Neale, reveals a significant difference between those sermons and the ones edited by Ross. The sermons by Boniface, Bede, Peter Damian, and Anselm, though certainly not lacking in eloquence, disclose an entirely different approach to preaching. Anselm, for example, preached by taking the gospel lesson for the day and expounding it verse by verse; Peter Damian seldom took a text at all, but opened his sermon without one and followed his own personal practices. The relative formlessness of the older sermons is in direct contrast to the more structured sermons of the later university clerics. It is this type of sermon, then, one which reflects a formal but not inflexible structure, that we should examine. Thus, in analyzing the Pardoner's Tale in relation to this "modern" medieval sermon we need to ask two questions. First, does the tale exhibit an analogous structure, the parts of which are developed by rhetorical techniques similar to those used by the medieval sermon maker? Secondly, does the tale reveal the close relationship between "sentence" and form so characteristic of the late medieval sermon?

II

A breakdown of the Pardoner's Tale clearly reveals structural parts quite similar to those posited by Basevorn and Waleys in their treatises. The main elements and their location in the tale are as follows:

333–334	Theme
335–462	*Protheme:* Prologue. The Pardoner's Confession.
463–482	*Introduction to the theme.* Introduction to the Flanders tavern scene.
483–660	*Division, subdivision and discussion of the theme.*
661–894	*The major exemplum:* the rioters' search for death.
895–915	*Recapitulation and "application."* Repeats the sins and asks that "God forgeve yow youre trespas."

(line numbers conform with F. N. Robinson, 2d ed.)

The subdivisions are as follows:

483–504	*Drunkenness*
505–588	*Gluttony*
589–628	*Gambling*
629–659	*Swearing*

Despite Charles Shain's assertion that there is no theme in the Pardoner's Tale, the Pardoner clearly states "My theme is alwey oon, and evere was— / *Radix malorum est Cupiditas.*'' The difficulty occurs, apparently, following the Pardoner's announcement. Carleton Brown claims that the Pardoner does not preach on his announced theme but shifts, instead, to the "tavern scene," which is unprepared for. But there is something far more important at this juncture in the prologue: there is the self-exposé of the Pardoner himself, the direct antithesis of what one might expect from a representative of the Church. What we must recognize is that the prologue is an integral part of the Pardoner's sermon and cannot be separated from it. Far from being merely "reported" to the pilgrims, it is deliberately preached to them, and the fact that it is a confession does not affect the structural order of the sermon.

Since the confession of the Pardoner follows the theme, it may serve as a protheme. Wenzel's assertion that he has never seen an actual sermon use self-revelation as a protheme assumes a fixed purpose and defines self-revelation in very narrow terms. While not necessarily confessing his sins to the audience, the preacher quite customarily in the protheme either declared his unworthiness or attacked the unworthy in his profession: "But notwithstandynge, it is full herde for me, for I knowe my-selfe vnabull and not sufficiente for to do þis dede." In listing the sins of his fraternity, the Pardoner simply individualizes the usually general attacks on his profession. *He* becomes the unworthy preacher, and the usual moral admonition against such preachers becomes a compelling drama of sinfulness in action. Stephen Langton seems to anticipate both Chaucer's Pardoner and his theme in one of his sermons addressed to an audience of clerics:

> The delight of the Lord ought to be the clerical order and especially the priesthood. . . . You are the ones who are entrusted with dispensing the ineffable sacrament of the body and blood of the Lord. . . . The root of all things is cupidity, as the apostle says (I Tim. 6:10). But although it is reprehensible in anyone at all, it is detestable in a priest. There are, nevertheless, certain priests who turn the sacrament of the altar into a quest for worldly profit.

According to the writers of the *artes praedicandi,* the protheme must follow the theme, but as Smyth indicates, it may serve many purposes:

> The ante-theme [protheme] should always be kept short: and the preacher must remember that here is his opportunity to captivate the attention, the good will, and the docility of his congregation. This may be done in several ways: for example, says Basevorn, he may strike their imagination, whether by narrating some authentic marvel or prodigy of nature, or by disclosing the explanation of some well-known fact. . . . [He] may alarm them by some terrible narrative . . . , he may make emphatically clear to his hearers that he is out for their souls, and not . . . their money. . . . Waleys adds that if the preacher in his ante-theme touches upon the qualities required in a preacher . . . , he should do it . . . briefly.
>
> (*The Art of Preaching*)

This passage is especially significant in relation to what the Pardoner says. What could fulfill Basevorn's explanation of a well-known fact better than the Pardoner's revelation of the misuse of sermons: "For certes, many a predicacioun / Comth ofte tyme of yvel entencioun"? (ll. 407–8). And what better way to "captivate" the attention or the "good will" of the Canterbury Pilgrims than to relate some intimate segment from one's life?

The dramatic power of personal confession, especially in the Christian Church, is attested to by hundreds of instances ranging from Augustine to Billy Sunday, who often used personal confession to draw thousands of people, many of whom had not the slightest interest in salvation. The Pardoner's confession has the same function. What the Pardoner lacks, of course, are the other obligations required of the penitent—contrition, and satisfaction—as listed in the Parson's "foure condiciouns" for a "trewe and a profitable confessioun." But those are less dramatic and of little interest to most of the company. The important point finally is that the prologue (protheme) does not violate the structure of the medieval sermon; it deliberately adumbrates the content.

The protheme in the "modern" medieval sermon often terminates in a prayer, followed by a repetition of the theme both for the purpose of stressing the text and "for the possible arrival of latecomers." The Pardoner does not have a prayer, but as Ross indicates, the disagreement of Waleys over the introduction to the theme renders the whole progression ambiguous. He adds:

Prothemes which do not end with prayer cannot be distinguished from introductions to themes unless the sermon contains both protheme and introduction. In this case, the section which precedes the introduction and which ends with a repetition of the main theme cannot be anything other than a protheme, though it no longer serves its original purpose.

Also an examination of the sermons in Ross's collection reveals that two which are classed as "modern" or university sermons do not contain prayers, although both contain prothemes and introductions.

The next element in our order is the introduction of the theme. As Ross states, the purpose of the introduction "seems to have been to afford the preacher an opportunity to catch the attention of his audience and to make clear his purpose." Smyth demonstrates that it may begin in various ways, with either a quotation from Scripture, a popular proverb, or some observation by the preacher himself. Moreover, it may be either narrative or argumentative, it may be an analogy or even an exemplum. The only restriction seems to be that it should explain the meaning of or provide a key to the theme.

If we examine the so-called "tavern sins" in the first lines following the prologue of the Pardoner's Tale (463ff.), we may readily see that they do meet the criterion for an introduction. The Pardoner begins with a short exemplum—"In Flaundres whilom was a compaignye"—which not only allows him to "catch the interest of his audience," but which also smoothly effects transition to the division of his theme which follows. It is the type of sins listed—gluttony, blasphemy, gaming—or their order that is usually offered as "proof" the Pardoner's sermon lacks unity. But a close look at these sins reveals a unity that is striking in its subsequent application. In the first place, as Alfred Kellogg points out in his interpretation of the tale, the Pardoner is speaking of *cupiditas* in the Augustinian sense, as sin in the most general terms—the opposite of *caritas*. As Kellogg notes:

> All the sins treated in the Pardoner's sermon—gluttony, lechery, gaming, blasphemy, homicide—are, in the pattern of the seven deadly sins, connected with the central theme of avarice. Gluttony and lechery are linked, as the Pardoner piously notes . . . and in the scheme of the seven deadly sins they follow in order from avarice.

Morton Bloomfield also notes the increasing popularity of avarice: "In the later Middle Ages avarice gained increasing emphasis as the cause of all sin, but it did not replace pride officially because by that time the Sins had official status."

Not only, then, does the "tavern scene" serve as an introduction to the Pardoner's theme of avarice, it also allows him to progress to the next element of the "modern" medieval sermon—the division of the theme into its constituent parts: gluttony to lechery to "dronkenesse," the last of which Bloomfield defines as a "branch of gluttony" itself:

> And right anon thanne comen tombesteres
> Fetys and smale, and yonge frutesteres,
> Syngeres with harpes, baudes, wafereres,
> Whiche been the verray develes officeres
> To kyndle and blowe the fyr of lecherye,
> That is annexed unto glotonye.
> The hooly writ take I to my witnesse
> That luxurie is in wyn and dronkenesse.
>
> (ll. 477–84)

Moreover, the introduction allows the Pardoner to subdivide the theme into the related parts that Kellogg spoke of—gambling, blasphemy, and homicide—all of which are developed in their turn, the first two in the body of the sermon (ll. 590–628; 629–59), and the last in the long exemplum.

Thus the two elements, the division and subdivision, appear in sharp outline in the Pardoner's sermon. Moreover, the methods of developing the various elements are faithfully observed. As Charland, Ross, and Smyth remind us, each member of the division must be confirmed by biblical or other authority. The subdivision "dronkenesse" is confirmed by the story of Lot (l. 485), gluttony is confirmed by the story of Adam, and a significant quotation from St. Paul:

> "Mete unto wombe, and wombe eek unto mete,
> Shal God destroyen bothe," as Paulus seith.
>
> (ll. 522–23)

Swearing is confirmed by a quotation from Jeremiah:

> The heighe God forbad sweryng at al,
> Witnesse on Mathew; but in special
> Of sweryng seith the hooly Jeremye,
> "Thou shalt swere sooth thyne othes, and nat lye,
> And swere in doom, and eek in rightwisnesse."
>
> (ll. 633–37)

Only in gambling does the Pardoner fail to confirm scripturally, and there he carefully confirms by "Stilboun," "This wise philosophre" (l. 620). Not only are these divisions delineated correctly, there is also some evidence that the Pardoner attempts to enunciate the words of the divisions according to the traditional fashion. Basevorn insisted that the thematic divisions must terminate in syllables that have similar sounds (*consimilis terminatio dictionum*), and he gave an example: *statum, actum,* and *modum.* Is it purely by chance that all but one of the Pardoner's division-words—"hasardrye," "glotonye," "lecherye," "dronkenesse"—seem to follow this rule?

Not only does the Pardoner's sermon adhere to the principal divisions of the "modern" medieval sermon structure, but it also follows many of the rhetorical methods of development, what Charland calls "*Les Autres Ornements.*" There were dozens of these ornaments, some of which had fixed places in the sermon, and others of which could be used anywhere the preacher thought necessary. Some of the more important ones mentioned by Basevorn and Waleys are: *digressio, correspondentia, circulatio, unitio, allusio,* and *repetitio. Digressio,* as Charland informs us, "is a development beyond the main subject. It has no fixed place in the sermon." The Pardoner employs this figure in several places. One such is in the discussion of gluttony, where he also uses another rhetorical device of "marking the opposite" (that is, defining gluttony by abstinence):

> But herkneth, lordynges, o word, I yow preye,
> That alle the sovereyn actes, dar I seye,
> Of victories in the Olde Testament,
> Thrugh verray God, that is omnipotent,
> Were doon in abstinence and in preyere.
> Looketh the Bible, and ther ye may it leere.
>
> (ll. 573–78)

Correspondentia consists merely in further subdividing one of the principal divisions without bothering to confirm it, in order to reveal its more pervasive nature or its subsequent effects. In speaking of gambling, the Pardoner says:

> Now wol I yow deffenden hasardrye.
> Hasard is verray mooder of lesynges,
> And of deceite, and cursed forswerynges,
>
> . . . .
>
> It is repreeve and contrarie of honour.
>
> (ll. 590–92, 595)

Circulatio is a much more complex patterning of divisions, an interweaving of minor subdivisions which adds unity to *correspondentia*. The Pardoner, of course, does this with his reference to wine ("dronkenesse") in the section on gluttony (l. 549), but the precise order cannot be determined. *Unitio,* however, which Charland defines as an ornament that sums up "in one phrase or one word the ideas which have been successively developed" is clearly evident in both location and function:

> O cursed synne of alle cursednesse!
> O traytours homycide, O wikkednesse!
> O glotonye, luxurie, and hasardrye!
> Thou blasphemour of Crist with vileynye
> And othes grete, of usage and of pride!
>
> (ll. 895–99)

Allusio is also obvious. It is sometimes used in referring to biblical authority or to biblical or legendary heroes ("Sampsoun, Sampsoun"). *Repetitio* may be repetition of words or phrases, and one of the most significant examples occurs in an allusion to Lemuel: "What was comaunded unto Lamuel— / Nat Samuel, but Lamuel, seye I" (ll. 584–85).

III

The Pardoner's Tale reflects the medieval sermon structure both in its general design, the relation of the parts to the whole, and in the methods of developing those parts. But it reflects still another vital principle indicative of the late medieval sermon—the relation of theme to form. Charland asserts that the sermon makers from the beginning insisted "on the fundamental role of the theme in relation to the rest of the sacred discourse." The theme was the root of the sermon tree, and "as every tree grows from the roots, every sermon proceeds from the theme, which contains all the matter." In all of the "modern" sermons in Ross's collection the words of the theme are carried throughout the sermon, appearing in the subsequent protheme, introduction to the theme, division of the theme, and the discussion. Whatever the method of development—through analogies, reference to authorities, comparisons, examples—the theme is held constantly before the audience by the preacher. In number 51, the theme, "*Ave, gracia plena*," is echoed by the protheme, where Mary is "qwene of heven" and "all erthe is full of hure praysyng." The repetition of the theme is given in both Latin and English ("Hail, full of grace"). In the introduction she is contrasted to Eve, who "founde synne and sorowe"; Mary "founde swetnesse and grace" which led Gabriel to say "Haill, full of grace." The introduction ends with a repetition: " 'Haill, full of grace,' as I seid at þe begynnyng." In the division the words of the theme—again repeated—are used to provide a physical and moral description of the Virgin: she is "semely in sighte," "semely in lovynge," and "wurthy of gretyng" (hailing). In the discussion various examples are used to develop the theme, including examples of hypocritical hailing: Judas, who when he met Christ said, " 'Ave rabi'; et osculatus est eum''; and Joab, who hailed Amasa only to kill him. The sermon concludes with a quotation from Paul "Vbi habundauit delict[um, superbundauit] gracia," and a reminder that though man fell through woman he is now saved by another.

In the Pardoner's Tale the theme of avarice with its attendant sins—gluttony, blasphemy, drinking, lechery—is consistently delineated by the Pardoner. The theme is illustrated in five different sections of the tale: the theme in general, the prologue (protheme), the introduction of the theme, the body of the sermon, and the exemplum. Moreover, it is summarized at the end, in the *unitio*.

In the prologue, the protheme that prepares for the body of the sermon, the Pardoner's confession reflects the sins of avarice—gluttony, blasphemy, drinking, lechery:

> I wol have moneie, wolle, chese, and whete,
> Al were it yeven of the povereste page,
> Or of the povereste wydwe in a village,
> Al sholde hir children sterve for famyne.

> Nay, I wol drynke licour of the vyne,
> And have a joly wenche in every toun.
>
> (ll. 448–53)

In the introduction of the theme, the sins are reiterated in the short exemplum "Of yonge folk that haunteden folye, / As riot, hasard, stywes, and tavernes, / . . . And eten also and drynken over hir myght" (ll. 464–65, 468). This exemplum is a minor dramatization of the sins and serves as a prelude to the major exemplum that follows the discussion. As such, it enables the Pardoner to get to the tavern sins—the specific sins of avarice—quickly and smoothly.

In the body of the sermon the individual sins are developed by division and discussion as already indicated. Each sin is confirmed by proper authority, and each is associated with an exemplum that clearly illustrates the danger of sin.

The sins of avarice appear once more in the long exemplum, now in dramatic form. The rioters freely make oaths on "Goddes armes," "Goddes digne bones," and "Goddes precious dignitee." And the plot to kill the youngest rioter, as one of the plotters says, is necessary so that "we bothe oure lustes all fulfille, / And pleye at dees right at oure owene wille" (ll. 833–34).

Finally, at the end of the sermon, the sins of avarice are repeated for the last time in the *unitio,* which Robinson terms the "recapitulation" (ll. 895–99). The *unitio,* however, does more than simply recap the sins that have been developed and dramatized. It punctuates the last link in the tightly controlled structure of the Pardoner's sermon.

It seems clear at this point that we should reevaluate the sermon in the Pardoner's Tale. It *is* a sermon, carefully unified, and quite similar structurally to the university, or "modern" sermons previously referred to. It can be classified neither as a homily, an "older, freer form," nor as a purely formal exercise, the *sermo examinatorius.* It is a representative example of late medieval sermons.

The Pardoner and the Word of Death

R. A. Shoaf

This book concludes with an analysis of the Pardoner's Prologue and Tale, for several reasons, some more obvious than others. Most obvious is that the Pardoner of all Chaucer's posers is the most skillful, theatrical, and elusive. Only slightly less obvious is the connection in the Pardoner and his discourse between language and money. He is obsessed with both and uses the one as a magnet for the other: " 'Of avarice and of swich cursednesse / Is al my *prechyng*, for to make hem free / To yeven hir *pens*' " (C. 400–402, F. N. Robinson, 2d ed.; emphasis added). Then there is the emphasis on "entente," this word so insistent in Chaucer's vocabulary: not only does it occur three times (ll. 403, 423, 432), but the problem which revolves around it is vivid in the Pardoner's claim that " 'though myself be a ful vicious man / A moral tale yet I yow telle kan' " (ll. 459–60). Here is an open breach between intent and content, and the emergent crisis of reference demands attention and scrutiny. Next, less obvious but no less important than these other reasons, is the insistence on buying and especially on the buying of the Redemption. On three occasions the Pardoner recurs to the "buying again" which Christ's sacrifice effected, and twice he uses the exact phrase "boght agayn," as if the etymology of "redemptio" held some sort of magical power for his own personal redemption (C. 501, 766, 902). Answering to this insistence on the Redemption is

From *Dante, Chaucer, and the Currency of the Word: Money, Images, and Reference in Late Medieval Poetry.* © 1983 by Pilgrim Books.

Herry Bailly's pointed remark, just before he calls on the Pardoner, about Virginia of the Physician's Tale: " 'Allas, to deere *boughte* she beautee!' " (C. 293; emphasis added). In addition, there is the large and almost oppressive fact, if also usually implicit, that the Pardoner's audiences as a rule "buy" his words—his, so to speak, "pitch"— when he wins pence from them (see C. 403–4). The Pardoner's desire for personal redemption, I think we can suggest, is, in fact, displaced and materialized in the purchase of him which his audiences make when they buy his words.

The manner of this displacement is crucial to understanding the Pardoner and the crisis of reference; in fact, it relates to the final and perhaps most important reason for concluding [*Dante, Chaucer, and the Currency of the Word*] with the Pardoner, or the agon in his prologue and tale between the literal and the allegorical. Commentary on this and related matters is by now very extensive. Here I make no pretense to the last word and certainly no attempt at a summary of all the previous words. I do propose, however, to open the question of the letter and the spirit from the position which [*Dante, Chaucer, and the Currency of the Word*] has so far mapped out. In particular, I will argue that, if the Merchant's allegory is counterfeit, the Pardoner's is, on the contrary, true; and the truth in which he deals, I will go on to argue, is what makes him so dark and ominous a figure. He is a liar, a consummate liar, who nonetheless deals in the truth, and deals in it even to the point of truly confessing that he lies. This mixture of truth and lies resembles the mixture of life and death in the Pardoner. For a lie is the word of death. Recall that the Father of lies (John 8:44) brought death into the world (Sap. 2:24); and "when the Devil speaks a lie, he speaks from his own" (John 8:44), and just so the Pardoner "from his own speaks" (from his own "proper") when he lies. But when he lies, his word of death is a very live word, having its own strange efficacy. Hence the word of death (a lie) is the death of the word—but while it still lives. And is this not the Pardoner? A living death?

The Pardoner recurs to the Redemption twice in his own voice, once in that of the Old Man. The first time he is castigating gluttony (ll. 500–504):

> O original of oure dampnacioun,
> Til Crist hadde boght us with his blood agayn!

> Lo, how deere, shortly for to sayn,
> Aboght was thilke cursed vileynye!
> Corrupt was al this world for glotonye.

The second time, at the end of the tale, he is attacking the "cursed synne of alle cursednesse" (ll. 900–903):

> Allas! mankynde, how may it bitide
> That to thy creatour, which that the wroghte
> And with his precious herte-blood thee boghte,
> Thou art so fals and so unkynde, allas?

Finally, the Old Man, as he directs the revelers to Death, says (ll. 765–67):

> "Se ye that ook? Right there ye shal hym fynde.
> God save yow, that boghte agayn mankynde,
> And yow amende."

Note in passing that in the first example the Pardoner uses "bought" twice ("Aboght was thilke cursed vileynye"); and I suspect that the point he is suggesting is that, as Adam dearly bought damnation, so Christ in turn bought us back from damnation, just as dearly. In good homilectic fashion he is alluding to the doctrine of first and second Adam, so emphasized by Saint Paul. But whether or not he is, in fact, flourishing his preacher's skill in this way, certainly the notion of buying holds some special importance for him. And we can trace this importance to its source in his longing for personal redemption, a longing which is part of a personality at once desperately incomplete and unbearably brilliant.

That the Pardoner's personality is incomplete should need no arguing: he is a "geldyng" or a "mare" (A. 691). But the amount of ink spilled in arguing anyway over these words and their implications cannot go unnoticed. Some say that the Pardoner is a *eunuchus ex nativitate;* some say that he is a homosexual; some say that he is a hermaphrodite; some say that the question is open; and Donaldson says that "the fact seems to be that there is good evidence that the Pardoner is and is not homosexual, and you may read him either way you please, with perfect confidence that you are probably wrong." I say that all this is beside the point, the point being that the Pardoner's identity is a question to others, such as Chaucer the pilgrim, and therefore almost certainly a question to himself. To this extent, then, he is incomplete.

That the Pardoner is also an unusually brilliant man would seem evident from his skill with words: he delivers a sermon which is a model of rhetorical finesse. An incomplete but brilliant man is likely to suffer wrenching emotions and as a consequence to be abnormally sensitive. Chaucer has a number of ways of suggesting this abnormal sensitivity. At this point I want to call attention to the one which I consider most important, the Pardoner's position in the General Prologue.

He comes last among the portraits. To be sure, Herry is described after the Pardoner (at ll. 751–57), but in introducing the last five of his "compaignye," the last of whom is the Pardoner, Chaucer goes out of his way to remark, "there were namo" (l. 544). Hence, obviously, Chaucer must have consciously placed the Pardoner last. Now in itself the Pardoner's position might indicate some special emphasis but no more. In opposition to the first position, however, and the figure who holds it, the Knight, it does considerably more than that. The Knight and the Pardoner form a polarity of far-reaching significance, especially since it is the Knight who attempts to reconcile Herry and the Pardoner at the end of the latter's sermon. The Knight, in contrast to the Pardoner, enjoys the highest social status of the pilgrims; moreover, as a crusader, he is a valuable servant of the church, though he has taken no orders as far as we know and obeys no direct mandate from Rome; his great piety seems obvious from his haste to go on the pilgrimage; and he is definitely masculine since he has fathered a son—no question about his identity. All these characteristics, and doubtless others one could name, suggest a positive to which the Pardoner is a negative. And yet Chaucer never leaves anything so simple as all that. From the tale which the Knight tells—where order is so stifling it is a kind of disorder, where a soldierly Stoicism fills out an ostensibly Christian mold, where an old man's weary wisdom disconcertingly recommends a bloodless and a dubiously Christian resignation, where the highest human achievement is the pagan and heroic, hardly Christian, ideal of good fame after death (A. 3047–49), and where passion is cynically laughed at (A. 1785–1814)—from all this it is possible to conclude that the Knight is one of the least passionate and most rigid men whom Chaucer ever imagined. To *this* negative the Pardoner is a certain though highly problematic positive, and this is principally why Chaucer positions his portrait last. With his vivid imagination, powers of projection, and ability to identify with roles, the Pardoner could never, for example, take such a mechanical and coldly matter-of-fact position on Arcite's death as does the Knight when he describes the dissolution of the latter's body (A. 2743–60, especially 2759–60: "And certeinly, ther Nature wol nat wirche, / Fare wel phisik! go ber the man to chirche!"). The Pardoner would give as vivid a description, if not one more vivid; but he would entertain none of the Knight's clinical pedantry or any of his soldierly brusqueness—he would feel more of what he was saying and communicate more of that feeling. Thus he and his position counterpoise the Knight and his in order to suggest the significant difference between them, or the Pardoner's capacity for feeling.

The Pardoner's capacity for feeling, I perhaps should note, is hardly the same thing as sympathy; it is, quite the contrary, more like abnormal sensitivity. And in this condition the Pardoner suffers his mutilated personality morbidly. He is not whole, and he knows it; moreover, the community in which he must live can include him only by ostracizing him. And yet, brilliant as he is, he must have an abstract appreciation of what it would be like to be whole and to belong—he can imagine it, for imagination is supremely if also pervertedly his gift. And in his imagination would be borne the longing for personal redemption, such as Christ holds out to man, and thence would arise the obsession with buying. He keeps coming back to that possibility which he knows he can never enjoy.

It is important to this argument that Christianity, both before and during Chaucer's day, emphasized the element of "purchase" in the Redemption. Saint Augustine may be considered representative: "Behold, Christ has suffered; behold, the Merchant shows us the payment; behold the price which he paid: his blood is poured out."

This example could be supplemented by many others from the patristic and later medieval periods. More important for the moment, however, is to set the emphasis on purchase and debt in its wider scriptural context. It goes back to Paul (1 Cor. 6:20, for example) and ultimately to Christ himself (Matt. 13:44–46, for example). Christ and Paul are also responsible, in different ways, for the fundamental notion supporting the Pardoner's vocation, or the selling of pardons. For these pardons derive ultimately from the treasury of merit which Christ's sacrifice and that of his saints established in and for the church. Strictly speaking, the church dispenses to the Pardoner merit from its superabundant store, and he, in turn, sells this merit in the form of pardons for a profit which is indisputably illicit in his case. Buying and selling, credit and debit, merchandising, are structured into everything the Pardoner says and does; and they are as much a part of the legitimate church as they are a part of his illegitimate desires and deeds.

A ravaged personality, mutilated; a brilliant mind, unbalanced; abnormal sensitivity; a probable desire to be saved, to be redeemed, precisely because of such deformity; a profession which involves merchandising out of the store of the Redemption and the treasury of Christ. The pattern of the obsession should be clear by now.

According to Saint Augustine, men "were able to sell themselves, but they were not able to redeem themselves." The Pardoner, I am suggesting, is well aware of this. He sells himself, his act, every day in his profession; but, to judge from the pattern of his obsession, he knows because he regrets that he cannot buy himself back. Only the Other can redeem. Hence his unmistakable but also nervous delight in duping his audiences: by means of his poses and impostures he wins their pence. In a very "literal" or "carnal" or material sense, they purchase him, and this purchase is a surrogate for the Redemption he can never otherwise have. Although I have used the word "literal" here, its precise application is problematical; and we will need to return again and again to the problematic of the "literal." Already we can see one element in it. If the Merchant is a "proprio-loquist," always seeking his own meaning of meaninglessness, the Pardoner, on the contrary, is an "alieniloquist" because he needs and he craves the Other and others:

> What results is the "vertige du même," the fear or the blank awareness that comes when you realize that you are only one, that you do not have the colorful interest of variety about you, that there was only yourself to deal with all the time. With this recognition, with the lack of a genuine "other," you collapse into nothingness. Hence the myth of the suicide of Narcissus, the meeting in sameness that extinguishes the tautological consciousness.
>
> (Irving Massey, *The Gaping Pig: Literature and Metamorphosis*)

In order to escape his "tautological consciousness," the Pardoner desperately seeks the Other: hence the coruscation, the torrent, of meanings he releases in his prologue and tale—he never stops talking until Herry shuts him up.

But at the same time, all the meanings, we suspect, do somehow serve the letter; somehow they are carnal and material. Instead of the blood with which Christ redeemed man, the Pardoner desires the coin of his audiences. Instead of the sacrament which "effects what it signifies" because the blood of Christ instituted it, the Pardoner desires "real" money whose tangibility and materiality solace him and whose efficacy is visible and present. For the efficacy that is invisible and intangible, the Pardoner substitutes the materiality of purchasing power. Where the pardon he preaches is sacramental, immaterial, and invisible, but efficacious for the faithful, the Pardoner himself is relentlessly carnal and material. And this because his faith, like his body, is sterile: it exists, but it bears no fruit.

My concern here is the connection between the Pardoner's sexual and spiritual conditions. Whatever the former is said to be, there can be no doubt that the Pardoner is physically sterile. Now from this condition, some have reasoned that he is also spiritually sterile. And I agree that he is, even as I also doubt such reasoning. I doubt it because the Pardoner does in fact produce (C. 429–33; emphasis added):

> "But though myself be gilty in that synne,
> *Yet kan I maken oother folk to twynne*
> *From avarice,* and soore to repente.
> But that is nat my principle entente;
> I preche nothyng but for coveitise."

The Pardoner saves souls, or at least he claims that he does. He is doubtless boasting, but boasting is usually an exaggeration of fact, and given the Pardoner's powers at preaching, it is not difficult to concede the probable fact that he has saved *some* people from avarice. The Pardoner does, then, probably produce fruit, or good works, through the seminal power of his verbal art. But he is himself, as has rightly been said, sterile because he does not believe in this fruit; he has no faith in its efficacy—he has, as he says, a different intent. The Pardoner has no faith, though he certainly knows in the abstract what faith is, because his intent is "nothyng but for coveitise." Between him and the efficacy of the word, blocking that efficacy for him, is a covetous intent, like a dead body across the way.

The Pardoner *does* good works, he *is* sterile and faithless. So much is in keeping with his role of actor or poser or impostor: nothing in himself, he can play anyone or anything. Between his act and his "self" falls his "yvel entencioun" (l. 408) to "wynne gold and silver" (l. 440). Hence, of any simplistic theory of the instrumentality of words the Pardoner will make a mockery. His words are almost always duplicitous. And in the "yvel entencioun" where this duplicity arises is the failed reference of the Pardoner's "dead" or sterile body.

The Pardoner lives in a body that has no referent. He is not really a man, not really a woman, and if he is both, he is neither—in fact, as we say of animals, he is *neutrum,* or neuter. And this I take to be the importance of Chaucer the pilgrim's doubt, "geldyng *or a* mare" (A. 691; emphasis added)—the Pardoner is *neither* this *nor* that. *In* his body, consequently, the Pardoner can refer to all sorts of things; *with* his body, however, he can refer to nothing (not even to pleasure, I suspect, since a man who could enjoy pleasure would not dirty it the way the Pardoner does). Sterile and thus without reference with his body, the Pardoner must rely on the surrogate seed of language, in something like the same way an actor relies on the costumes and props attending a role. This surrogate seed is obviously as much a fishwife's or a sailor's or Herry Bailly's as it is the Pardoner's; and this must gall him, wound his pride. Nevertheless, it is fertile; it does produce. It produces, however, not the Pardoner's property but the converted souls of others. And the Pardoner is dependent on this creativity. Without it, he could not fulfill his "yvel entencioun." With it, he works roughly as follows. He lets the seed of language (or the seed of the signs which are his relics) inseminate others with conversion, but he charges them for it so that, as language converts them, they convert language or seed into money which then "inseminates" and "fertilizes" as it "redeems" the Pardoner and his "dead" body. Words become seeds, seeds become money, and money becomes seeds to fill the Pardoner with the sexuality and fertility which he otherwise lacks. Hence the "yvel entencioun" and duplicitous reference can accurately be said to originate in the Pardoner's "dead" body. The desire to "quicken" that body gives rise to them both.

Because of his sexual deformity, the Pardoner indulges an "yvel entencioun" which eventuates in a "literal" or "carnal" acceptation of signs. Instead of spiritual redemption, he desires the "literal" purchase which audiences make when they pay him for preaching. But this "literalism," we can see, is peculiar: it depends, in fact, on metaphoricity. We must never forget the Pardoner's manifest intelligence. He knows that he cannot be spiritually redeemed because he is in a state of sin. He also knows (he is too self-conscious a poser not to know) that he is playing a game with his audiences and their pence. Hence he probably also knows that he wants and accepts their hard cash because metaphorically as well as literally it is redemptive. The Pardoner knows his metaphors—every poser must. And if he takes Christ's redemption "literally," reducing it to "real" coins, he covets "real" coins in part because of their metaphoricity in the theology of Redemption: their lure for him in part is that metaphoricity. Because Christ's saving work is understood in terms of purchase, merit, treasury, wealth, and so on, these and unrelated concepts and objects hold a special appeal for the Pardoner, who desires even as he resents and resists Christ's saving work. The Pardoner is a "literalist," yes, but to be a "literalist" in his case is to take metaphors very seriously. The word of death, to repeat, is a very live word.

Hence, one can argue that the Pardoner has a sort of faith—he takes metaphors seriously, and he believes that works are creative—and one can argue that he produces good works. But, and this is at the center of the tragedy he suffers and the terror he inspires, the works are not the product of the faith—they are the product rather of his "yvel entencioun" to "wynne gold and silver." Hence the Pardoner's faith is without works, and "even as the body without the spirit is dead, so also faith without works is dead" (James 2:26). The Pardoner's faith is like his body, his body like his faith—there but sterile, alive but dead, neuter and ready for any position. Neuter and ready for any position, the Pardoner obviously has no position of his own. Rather, he takes his position from the available cue. And in the present case, Herry Bailly provides the cue. He not only anticipates the Pardoner's obsession with buying but also suggests to him the two fundamental themes of his sermon, or Fortune and Nature. In "the wordes of the Hoost to the Phisicien and the Pardoner," Herry exclaims of Virginia, " 'Allas, to deere boughte she beautee!' " and then proceeds immediately to pontificate (C. 293–96; emphasis added):

> "Wherfore I seye al day that men may see
> That yiftes of *Fortune* and of *Nature*
> Been cause of deeth to many a creature."

Just so, the Pardoner proceeds to deliver a sermon whose central exemplum is a story very much involving the "yiftes of Fortune and of Nature." Moreover, and this is as important though perhaps less noticeable, these "wordes of the Hoost" begin with the statement that "Oure Hooste gan to swere as he were wood" (l. 287), and, of course, the Pardoner goes on to attack the sin of swearing in his sermon. Then, too, Herry introduces the " 'draughte of moyste and corny ale' " (l. 315), which spurs the Pardoner to abominate drunkenness. Finally, and of fundamental importance, Herry jargonizes with the Physician's profession (ll. 304–6):

> "I pray to God to save thy gentil cors,
> And eek thyne urynals and thy jurdones,
> Thyn ypocras, and eek thy galiones."

As Herry himself says, only too truly, he " 'kan nat speke in terme' " (l. 311). But by the attempt he inspires the Pardoner to pull out all the stops in his own jargon engine of preaching. Hence, when the "gentils" (l. 323) protest: " 'Nay, lat hym telle us of no ribaudye! / Telle us som moral thyng' " (ll. 324–25), the Pardoner obliges them by drawing, like the parasite he is, on their Host.

A parasite, with no position of his own, an actor and an impostor ready for any role, a neuter who is sterile, the Pardoner is both alive and dead. In fact, this is the way in which the very theology he exploits would characterize and analyze him. He himself shows us the way (ll. 542–43, 547–48; emphasis added):

> for they [cooks] caste noght awey
> That may go thurgh the golet softe and swoote.
>
> . . . .
>
> But, certes, *he that haunteth swiche delices*
> *Is deed, whil that he lyveth in tho vices.*

Every sinner, like the glutton, is dead while he lives in his vices (cf. Rom. 6:23). Of the Pardoner this is especially true since his body is "literally" dead as far as fertility is concerned. Hence theological analysis of the sinner and his condition realizes itself "literally" in the Pardoner: the *metaphor,* no less actual for that, of the sinner's living death is *literal* in the Pardoner. The Pardoner is literally a metaphor, the living death of sin—he is himself the word of death. At the same time, because the letter is not only dead but also "killeth" (2 Cor. 3:6), the Pardoner is metaphorically a letter: he figures in his body and in the use of his body the literalism which kills—he is also the death of the word. He is (once again the text draws us back to this formula) neuter: he is neither a metaphor nor a letter but a positionless mixture of both. He can pose as either and poses either as he will.

In fact, this—posing either indiscriminately—is the way in which he generates his sermon exemplum. It is a way much like the way in which cooks provide for a glutton's "wombe" (C. 534). He says (ll. 538–39):

> Thise cookes, how they stampe, and streyne, and grynde,
> And turnen substaunce into accident.

The Pardoner is himself a kind of cook: he boasts to the pilgrims that " 'in Latyn I speke a wordes fewe, / To *saffron* with my predicacioun' " (C. 344–45; emphasis added). His preaching is indeed a kind of stew of rhetorical sleights-of-hand. And he, like his culinary "scholastics," turns substance into accident: he reduces the substance of meaning into the accident of the letter or its carnal, material manifestation. The best brief example is his conversion of the Eucharist into its literal and material elements: " 'But first . . . heere at this alestake / I wol bothe *drynke,* and *eten* of a cake' " (C. 321–22; emphasis added). Although ale is not wine, eating and drinking just before preaching are obviously gestures reminiscent of the Eucharist. And the Pardoner doubtless intends to pose the *materials* of the sacrament (anything to eat and drink) as the *meaning* of the sacrament which most interests him.

So also with his exemplum. Here the best illustration is the revelers' boast that "this false traytour Deeth / . . . shal be slayn, he that so manye sleeth" (C. 699–700). While the text hardly needs scriptural exegesis to be interpreted, once interpreted, it profits from the context which exegesis provides. The revelers' words allude, of course, to Hosea 13:14, to which Saint Paul himself alludes in 1 Corinthians 15:55: "I will deliver them out of the hand of death. I will redeem them from death. O death, I will be thy death; O hell, I will be thy bite." The cry of the prophet, "O death, I will be thy death," exegesis consistently understands as the triumphant claim of Christ the Redeemer. It is He who will conquer Death or Hell or the Devil (ultimately one from the theological perspective) during his "descensus ad inferos" when He will liberate all those whom Death or Hell or the Devil think to hold in their power. The revelers, who number three probably in deliberate mockery of the Holy Trinity, are a drastically carnal version of the Triune Lord, and they are hardly likely to equal His victory in the struggle with Death. Indeed, they become the victims of Death instead of the victors precisely because they are so carnal. Scripture and its exegesis predict as much. In Hosea, after the outcry against death, the voice goes on: "Because he shall make a separation between brothers. The Lord will bring a burning wind that shall rise from the desert, and it shall dry up his springs, and shall make his fountain desolate; and he shall carry off the treasure of every desirable vessel." According to the commentaries, the one who "makes division among brothers" is the Devil or Hell or Death. Just so, when the three revelers were four, Death divided them by taking their "old felawe" (C. 672), whereupon the remaining three swore an oath of brotherhood together (as though each were the other's "owene ybore brother"; l. 704). But this brotherhood is destroyed in just the way in which Scripture and its commentaries suggest that it would be. When the youngest reveler decides to betray the other two, *"the feend,* oure enemy, / Putte in his thought that he sholde poyson beye" (ll. 844–45; emphasis added), and the result is precisely "division among brothers." The text consistently accords with what a contemporary would have expected from exegesis of this famous verse in Hosea. The Pardoner's allegory—almost, we might say, his allegorical method—is very neat and prim.

But he continues to serve the word of death. If his allegory reveals the fate of carnal men—of gluttons, gamblers, and oath-takers—it is, just so, an allegory about the carnal, about all those acts and features of carnality which so obsess the carnally frustrated Pardoner. Moreover, if his allegory is creative and fruitful, it nonetheless allows him once again to literalize the Redemption—if Christ's Redemptive work is the death of Death, the Pardoner's version of this work is the story of three youths who would literally kill Death. Once again the Pardoner has posed the metaphor of Redemption as literal: all the materials of the Redemption are here—a trinity, a tree, money (gold), death—to serve as the meaning of Redemption. And this pose is explicable, once again, in terms of his deformity and obsession. Himself "dead" and spiritually an "old man" (Rom. 6:6), he longs precisely for the death of Death, but for the literal death of Death. If Death literally died, then the "death" (of sterility) in his body might also die. He knows full well, I hasten to add, that this cannot be, but once again he takes the metaphor seriously. And he mixes metaphor and letter indiscriminately in a story about the death of Death. The death of Death *is* the promise to spiritual man: if a man dies to sin and the flesh, then he shall live (Rom. 6:3–11)—the life of the spirit. But the Pardoner does not want this life: he does not want to die—he is already dead. He wants rather the life of a virile, fertile body, and he wants the renewal of youth. Hence, necessarily, he longs for the literal death of Death. Just as his desire carnalizes or materializes the benefits of the Redemption, so it must also carnalize or materialize, literalize, the work of the Redemption, or the death of Death.

One other illustration of the Pardoner's "stew" of metaphor and letter will perhaps be of help. The Old Man directs the three revelers up a "croked wey" (C. 761) to a grove where he left Death "under a tree" (l. 763). Now it was under a tree that sin entered the world—the Tree of Knowledge of Good and Evil. It was *on* a tree—typologically and according to legend, the same tree—that Christ by His sacrifice conquered sin and destroyed Death. The metaphoricity of the tree where the three revelers, carnal parody of the Lord, will struggle with Death is manifest, even ostentatious. But this ostentatious metaphoricity only serves the greater triumph of the letter. For when this unholy trinity dies under/on the tree, Death—which is to be equated with the letter—consumes the metaphoricity itself as well as three foolish mortals. Death and its letter not only win the unholy trinity, they also win the *holy Trinity*. Death and its letter do not merely kill three men; they subvert the Crucifixion and the Redemption, "turning" their spiritual "substance" into the "accident" of three ordinary greedy men killing each other over "eighte busshels" (l. 771) of gold florins. Even as the event sets up the meanings, the very banality of the event undermines the meanings, and this is the way the Pardoner *intends* it: for him, the closest men get to redemption is a brief glorying over gold, then daggers and poison.

And this because he has himself failed of redemption. It is probably obvious by now that in the debate over the Pardoner's sudden *volte face* at the end of his sermon, I will incline to the old—and, I suppose, most would say, sentimentalized—view of Kittredge that he suffers a "paroxysm of agonized sincerity." While I disavow the late-nineteenth-century characterology implicit in this evaluation, and while I am sympathetic with the more modern position that the Pardoner is not a character at all but an instance of the illusoriness of self, I still maintain that the text asks us to hear a sudden reversal of positions. The crux is the word "leche" (C. 915–18; emphasis added):

> —And lo, sires, thus I preche.
> And Jhesu Crist, that is *oure soules leche,*
> So graunte yow his pardoun to receyve,
> For that is best; I wol yow nat deceyve.

Of course, the first problem is the "I wol yow nat deceyve": given his "yvel entencioun" to "wynne gold and silver" and his confession of hypocrisy—" 'Thus spitte I out my venym under hewe / Of hoolynesse, to semen hooly and trewe' " (C. 421–22)—it is difficult to believe that the Pardoner would ever will not to "deceyve"; it is difficult to believe that he would ever *take a position*—would ever expose himself as "himself" rather than as some imposture. But the same evidence—evidence of the lack of a self—can suggest, quite humanly and understandably so, the opposite conclusion. For a man of "yvel entencioun" and gross hypocrisy who " 'wol noon of the apostles countrefete' " (l. 447) is necessarily a man of acute self-consciousness. A poser always knows he is in a pose—that is the definition of a poser. And because of such knowledge, because of such self-consciousness, the Pardoner cannot but realize that he is sick, that he is moribund. His very obsession with Death and the Redemption also argues the same conclusion. Hence it only makes sense that he would at some point take that position, of all the positions in his neutrality he might take, which is the least possible, most tenuous, and yet desperately attractive to him—the position of "I want to be whole." So, for a moment, he admits, he poses (and takes the position) that Christ is the "leche" who makes whole, by means of his "pardoun." My point is not to sympathize with him but to understand him. He has enough intelligence to know the truth of what he has said. The actor or impostor can shift into truth just as easily as he can shift into a lie. Moreover, a neuter and a parasite who so desperately wants and needs healing would predictably refer to *the* Healer at some point, especially since he lives his life in carnal parody and imposture of the Healer—selling the latter's pardons to persons who are in fact from time to time healed. But the tragedy of such a poser is that he cannot hold this position for long; he knows his sickness too well—it has become almost comfortable for him. And so the Pardoner abandons "oure soules leche" and "his pardoun" so as to lapse back into the by now much more familiar role.

Hawking his pardons once again, the Pardoner confronts and affronts Herry Bailly (C. 941–45):

> "I rede that oure Hoost heere shal bigynne,
> For he is moost envoluped in synne.
> Com forth, sire Hoost, and offre first anon,
> And thou shalt kisse the relikes everychon,
> Ye, for a grote! Unbokele anon thy purs."

Much attention has been paid recently to the Pardoner's sexual affront of the Host. While I recognize the validity of this position, I am also intrigued by the *truth* of the Pardoner's accusation. Whether Herry is the *most* "envoluped in synne" we might want to debate, but *that* he is "envoluped in synne" we can hardly deny: he swears outrageously, drinks, indulges games of chance (the meal at his inn for which the pilgrims are contending), backbites his wife, (E. 2427–29), and gives in to rage. The Pardoner has read Herry very closely and read him very well. His intelligence continues awesome. The measure of how well he has read Herry is Herry's very rage. Herry reacts not only or most importantly to sexual effrontery but also and crucially to the bitter, sharp sting of truth. The Pardoner has penetrated the "envelope" ("envoluped in synne") of Herry's position or role or act—interpreted the *involucrum* of his position (and pose)—and this penetration *does* threaten Herry, not only sexually but also spiritually. Before the consummate actor his act is transparent. His envelope or covering or mask is like a set of easily decipherable codes for the master manipulator of codes.

Hence Herry's violence and attempt not only to penetrate the Pardoner's role but also to reduce him, to drag him down, to his positionless position, his sexless neutrality (C. 951–55):

> "But, by the croys which that Seint Eleyne fond,
> I wolde I hadde thy coillons in myn hond
> In stide of relikes or of seintuarie.
> Lat kutte hem of, I wol thee helpe hem carie;
> They shul be shryned in an hogges toord!"

Whatever the Pardoner's sexuality, Herry's threat to his "coillons" questions that sexuality and hence the Pardoner's identity. And the question is enough, enough to expose the pose of the consummate poser: "this Pardoner answerde nat a word; / So wrooth he was, no word ne wolde he seye" (ll. 956–57). At this moment the Pardoner is fixed in wrath, and it is the only position in which he can be fixed. "No word ne wolde he seye": of course not—words are the stuff of poses, and all poses have just been disposed of.

As the Knight of all the pilgrims occupies the most fixed position, so the Pardoner occupies the least. Indeed, it might be said that the opposition between the two in the General Prologue is that between fixed position (knight, soldier, noble, etc.) and no position at all. Therefore, when the Knight reconciles Herry and the Pardoner, a massive discrepancy opens up which in itself defines the Pardoner's tragedy. The very security of the Knight's and Herry's positions must oppress the Pardoner, who can only submit to the Knight's will because he has no position of his own. Exposed, the Pardoner disappears. In a kiss.

The importance of the Pardoner to *The Canterbury Tales,* if they are understood as a collection of the possible positions of poets and poetry, is that, consummate impostor, he occupies the extreme of "irreference." The Pardoner's very "self" is "counterfeit." If he " 'wol noon of the apostles countrefete,' " that is because they are apostles and not because he does not or is not "countrefete." If the Wife of Bath would substitute herself for the allegorical plenitude of Scripture and exegesis, like a heretic, if the Merchant would annihilate that plenitude because it accuses and condemns his own poverty, the Pardoner, on the contrary, revels in it because it is an inexhaustible supply of masks, feints, sleights-of-hand, and gimmicks—an inexhaustible supply of counterfeit selves. Unlike the Wife, who has a self (and such a self) to sell, or the Merchant, who has no self, only his craft, the Pardoner has a multiplicity of selves whenever he wants them—he is a broken mirror whose fragments reflect a brilliant but forever incomplete identity. And everything the Pardoner says or does is a frantic effort to collect the fragments in the ultimately vain attempt to say, "I am."

Hence the insistent and finally pathetic "self"-referentiality, itself only imposture: " 'for myn entente is nat but for to winne' " (C. 403). This declaration of his intent only proves the poverty of the Pardoner's content. In fact, it might plausibly be argued that the "character" of the Pardoner (understanding by the word "character" here the literary construct) is to be a character who has *only* a character. Chaucer, it may be, explores through the Pardoner the illusoriness of the boundary between inside and outside in phenomena so linguistic as "character." Any attempt to discover what makes the Pardoner tick, to get "inside" him, invariably meets with only more words, with only more "outside." The Pardoner seems continuously to transform content into intent, turning himself "inside out," through torrents of speech. Hence his "inside" is his "outside"; his "outside," his "inside." He is a "character" (itself only words) whose character is to be only words: we might subtitle his Prologue " 'Character' and Its Dis/Contents." Where the boundary between inside and outside is pure illusion, where there are only words on words, where there is only "character," the character (and we as well) are dis-contented. Where there is no content, there is no meaning to content. Where there are only words on words, there is only endless reference, never meaning. If reference is the "gold" of signs, then the Pardoner's gold is never minted. He never tells us what he means; or, if he does, as perhaps he does through the reference to Christ, "oure soules leche," he immediately takes it back—he is precisely *avaricious.* And just as the Old Man, probably a figure of avarice, is never understood, so is the Pardoner, "hoarding" *his* "meaning" or "content," never understood. And this because he only talks—it seems as if he could talk endlessly—and only talks so as to appropriate the coin of others to be *his* meaning, *his* content. His only content is his intent: coin, the coin of others—" 'nobles or pens, whiche that be goode and trewe' " (C. 930). Hence his poverty (and the poverty of the avaricious). Just enough of the moral sense of "goode and trewe" lingers in the monetary and commercial sense that it is possible to hear the pathetic irony: "goode and trewe" coin is as close as the Pardoner comes to the good and the true. Meaning for the Pardoner is coin, and coin is meaning: this is both extreme literalism and extreme metaphoricity, a "stew" of language. More important, it is an appropriation of meaning to the self and its desires which exploits community. The conversion of the substance of language into the accident of coin is a materialization of desire which exploits the community's need for media of exchange. It is a radical assertion of the priority of the private precisely there where the private should cooperate with the public if community is to exist and flourish. But the community, the household, of Christendom, unable to allow for the peculiar

privation of the Pardoner, will win no mercy from his relentless
desire to practice his privacy upon it.

And yet the poet, for whom the private is also prior, does not
thrive without a community. It is merely a vanity of romanticism
that the poet writes only for himself. The poet writes to be heard—
and thus *for* a community. At the same time, however, it is true that
the poem begins in the mind, "a fine and private place," and that
"the mind, In the act of finding what will suffice, destroys /
Romantic tenements of rose and ice" (Wallace Stevens, "Man and
Bottle"). The tremendous anxiety inscribed in the Pardoner is the
anxiety that from the mind to the community there is no translation—that the priority of the private in the world of art is absolute,
so that no reconstruction follows the destruction of the tenements.
And this is the anxiety that motivates even as it frustrates the
Pardoner's problematic confession. He goes out of his way to betray
his act and his pose to the pilgrims because he wants to involve them
in his act and his pose—he wants to establish with them a sort of
community of impostors, on his own terms. The Wife of Bath wants
to be an "auctoritee" in whatever community she happens to live in;
the Merchant does not give a damn about community; the Pardoner
wants a community of his own—and tries for it with the pilgrims.
For if they participate with him in his act and his pose, they thus
bestow upon him the self he otherwise lacks and cannot possess.
They make it possible for him to say "*I am* your pardoner"
(C. 931–34):

> "It is an honour to everich that is heer
> That ye mowe have a suffisant pardoneer
> T'assoille yow, in contree as ye ryde,
> For aventures whiche that may bityde."

I am not so naive as to think that the Pardoner's motives here are
pure; they obviously are not. But I do believe that his *im*pure motive
is the desire for an identity *as their pardoner*. In this regard, consider
the extraordinary word "suffisant": it suggests something more than
just "legitimate" or "authorized"; it suggests something like "I really
am adequate, you know," a sentiment in which conviction and
self-doubt keep uneasy company. The response which the Pardoner
is seeking is not only nor perhaps most importantly "nobles or pens"
but also something like "Yes, yes, well, tell us another—you really
are quite good at it." What he gets instead, though, is violence—

violence because words do refer and refer, moreover, to the truth. In the agonized privacy of his unredeemed (and just possibly unredeemable) self, the Pardoner, consummate impostor and artificer of roles and master of words though he be, has forgotten that words *always* refer. Herry Bailly's reaction is sufficient evidence of that. The word, even the word of death, refers. But words do not always or necessarily *translate* unless and until the community understands their intentionality and thus also their instrumentality.

If all instrumentality is narcissistic, then the Pardoner's is a narcissism so drastic as to be incapable of even an echo. He would have the pilgrims so completely suppose his pose that they can only oppose him. He would have them identify so far with him that they would end being he: he exposes his gimmick, works his gimmick, then asks them to buy his gimmick—all of which assumes that *they are one with him, do not differ from him.* But they are not one with him, and they do most certainly differ from him. The Pardoner, in short, has made no effort to translate. Rather he supposes that by exposing his pose he can impose upon the pilgrims a will to repose in him their trust. I recognize that this play of words is too much; I intend it so. It helps me to demonstrate the Pardoner's excess. To turn on the pilgrims, as he does, expecting them to buy his gimmick, the Pardoner must suppose *not* that they are his but that they are *he.* The Merchant, by contrast, supposes that the pilgrims will become his, his property—his creatures seeing the world as he sees it—and Herry Bailly almost obliges him. The Pardoner, however, supposes that the pilgrims are so completely one with him that they will obey him even as he obeys himself. Such a supposition, of course, is psychotic. It precludes any effort of translation—of taking the positions of others so as to see how they see the world. It is the supposition of one so accustomed to posing and imposture that he has forgotten that people are more than their poses.

Something Chaucer never forgot. We revere Chaucer precisely because he was a master of taking the positions of others so as to see how they see the world. The Pardoner, in contrast, is exclusively about himself. The exemplum he tells is about the old man he meets everyday in his own body. The Pardoner does not translate. When he chooses Herry to begin his pardoning, it is not only the fact that his words refer to the truth that so distresses Herry but also the fact that he supposes that there is no difference between Herry and him.

Truth and lie are horribly mixed. And the Pardoner is only talking to himself. Herry, of course, will have none of it—hence he fixes precisely on the most glaring difference between them when he talks back.

And people do talk back. Something else Chaucer never forgot.

Chronology

c. 1340–45	Geoffrey Chaucer born, probably in the wine-marketing area of London, Vintry Ward. His parents, Agnes and John Chaucer, are wealthy property owners; John is a prosperous London wine merchant.
1357	Chaucer serves as a page to Elizabeth de Burgh, Countess of Ulster.
1359–60	Chaucer serves in King Edward III's army in France. He is captured, but Edward pays his ransom.
c. 1366	Chaucer marries Philippa Roet. He begins his association with John of Gaunt, probably through his wife, whose sister, Katherine Swynford, is John of Gaunt's mistress. John Chaucer dies.
1367	As a member of King Edward III's household, Chaucer receives a royal annuity.
c. 1368–71	Writes *The Book of the Duchess*.
1372–73	Sent to Genoa and Florence in the service of the king, Chaucer probably becomes acquainted with the writings of Boccaccio, Petrarch, and Dante. He may also have met Petrarch.
c. 1372–80	Writes *Saint Cecilia,* which later becomes the Second Nun's Tale, and some of the Monk's tragedies.
1374	Chaucer moves to the house over the gate of Aldgate. Edward III appoints him Controller of the Customs and Subsidies on Wool for the port of London.
1377	Chaucer travels to France on the king's behalf.

159

	While he is there, Edward III dies and Richard II becomes king. Richard renews Chaucer's customs appointment and confirms his royal annuity.
1378	Richard II sends Chaucer to Milan, where he renews his acquaintance with Italian literature.
c. 1378–80	Writes *The House of Fame*.
1380	Cecilia Chaumpaigne sues Chaucer for *raptus*. He is cleared of all responsibility.
c. 1380–82	Writes *The Parliament of Fowls*.
1382–85	Chaucer is appointed Controller of the Petty Customs, but then begins to phase himself out of his customs jobs by appointing full-time deputies.
c. 1382–87	Chaucer translates Boethius's *Consolation of Philosophy* and writes *Troilus and Criseyde, Palamoun and Arcite* (the Knight's Tale), *The Legend of Good Women*, and other shorter works.
1385	Appointed Justice of the Peace for Kent.
1386	Chaucer is elected to Parliament as one of the two "Knights of the Shire" to represent Kent. He gives up his house at Aldgate and his controllerships.
1387	Philippa Chaucer dies. Chaucer loses his royal annuity and goes into debt. He travels to Calais.
c. 1387–92	Writes the General Prologue and the earlier of the *Canterbury Tales*.
1389	Richard II appoints Chaucer Clerk of the King's Works.
c. 1390–91	Chaucer oversees construction and repair on several buildings, including the Tower of London, Westminster Palace, and St. George's Chapel at Windsor Castle. Usually carrying substantial amounts of money, he is robbed several times and possibly is injured.
1391	Chaucer relinquishes his clerkship and is appointed deputy forester of the Royal Forest at North Petherton in Somerset.
c. 1391–93	Writes *A Treatise on the Astrolabe*.
c. 1392–95	Writes most of the *Canterbury Tales* during this period.
1394	Richard II grants Chaucer a new royal annuity.

c. 1396–1400   Chaucer writes the latest of the *Tales,* including probably the Nun's Priest's Tale and the Canon's Yeoman's Tale, and several other shorter poems.

1399   John of Gaunt dies. Later in the year, Richard II is deposed and killed; Henry IV becomes king. Henry confirms Chaucer's pension and grants him an additional annuity. Chaucer leases a house in the garden of Westminster Abbey.

1400   Chaucer dies, probably sometime between June and October, and is buried in Westminster Abbey.

Contributors

HAROLD BLOOM, Sterling Professor of the Humanities at Yale University, is the author of *The Anxiety of Influence, Poetry and Repression,* and many other volumes of literary criticism. His forthcoming study, *Freud: Transference and Authority,* attempts a full-scale reading of all of Freud's major writings. A MacArthur Prize Fellow, he is general editor of five series of literary criticism published by Chelsea House. During 1987–88, he served as the Charles Eliot Norton Professor of Poetry at Harvard University.

IAN BISHOP, Professor of English at the University of Bristol in England, is the author of *Chaucer's* Troilus and Criseyde, *A Critical Study.*

PENELOPE CURTIS has published on Pope, Yeats, and Chaucer.

DONALD R. HOWARD was Professor of English at Stanford University until his death in 1987. He is the author of *The Idea of the* Canterbury Tales and *Writers and Pilgrims: Medieval Pilgrimage Narratives and Their Posterity.* He also edited two volumes of Chaucer's poetry.

WARREN GINSBERG is Associate Professor of English at the State University of New York at Albany. He is the author of *The Cast of Character: The Representation of Personality in Ancient and Medieval Literature.*

H. MARSHALL LEICESTER, JR., Professor of English at the University of California at Santa Cruz, has written and published numerous articles on Chaucer, *Beowulf,* and the French Revolution.

MONICA E. MCALPINE is Professor of English at the University of Massachusetts. She is the author of *The Genre of* Troilus and Criseyde.

163

ROBERT P. MERRIX is Professor of English at the University of Akron. He has written many articles on Chaucer and Shakespeare.

R. A. SHOAF is Professor of English at the University of Florida. His books include *Dante, Chaucer, and the Currency of the Word* and *Milton, Poet of Duality*.

Bibliography

Baum, Paull F. *Chaucer: A Critical Appreciation*. Durham, N. C.: Duke University Press, 1958.

Beichner, Paul E. "Chaucer's Pardoner as Entertainer." *Mediaeval Studies* 25 (1963): 160–72.

Benson, C. David. *Chaucer's Drama of Style*. Chapel Hill: University of North Carolina Press, 1986.

Bolton, W. F. "Structural Meaning in the Pardoner's Tale and the Nun's Priest's Tale." *Language and Style* 11 (1978): 201–11.

Bronson, Bertrand H. *In Search of Chaucer*. Toronto: University of Toronto Press, 1960.

Brown, Carleton, ed. *The Pardoner's Tale*. London: Oxford University Press, 1935.

Calderwood, James L. "Parody in the Pardoner's Tale." *English Studies* 45 (1964): 302–9.

Chapman, Coolidge O. "The Pardoner's Tale: A Medieval Sermon." *MLN* 41 (1926): 506–9.

Condren, Edward I. "The Pardoner's Bid for Existence." *Viator* 4 (1973): 177–206.

Curry, Walter Clyde. *Chaucer and the Medieval Sciences*. New York: Barnes & Noble, 1960.

David, Alfred. "Criticism and the Old Man in Chaucer's Pardoner's Tale." *College English* 27 (1965): 39–44.

Dean, Christopher. "Salvation, Damnation, and the Role of the Old Man in the Pardoner's Tale." *The Chaucer Review* 3 (1968): 44–49.

Dempster, Germaine. "The Pardoner's Prologue." In *Sources and Analogues of Chaucer's* Canterbury Tales, edited by W. F. Bryan and Germaine Dempster, 409–14. New York: Humanities Press, 1958.

Donaldson, E. Talbot. "Chaucer's Three 'P's: Pandarus, Pardoner, and Poet." *Michigan Quarterly Review* 14 (1975): 282–301.

Dürmüller, Urs. "Sociolinguistics and the Study of Medieval English." In *Linguistic and Stylistic Studies in Medieval English*, edited by André Crépin, 5–22. Vol. 10. Paris: Publications de l'Association des Médievistes de l'Enseignement Supérieur, 1984.

Elliott, Ralph W. V. "Our Host's 'Triacle': Some Observations on Chaucer's Pardoner's Tale." *Review of English Literature* (Leeds) 7, no. 2 (April 1966): 61–73.

Faulkner, Dewey R., ed. *Twentieth-Century Interpretations of the Pardoner's Tale: A Collection of Critical Essays.* Englewood Cliffs, N. J.: Prentice-Hall, 1973.

Gallick, Susan. "A Look at Chaucer and His Preachers." *Speculum* 50 (1975): 456–76.

Gerould, Gordon H. *Chaucerian Essays.* Princeton, N. J.: Princeton University Press, 1952.

Gross, Seymour. "Conscious Verbal Repetition in the Pardoner's Prologue." *Notes and Queries* 198 (1953): 413–14.

Hallissy, Margaret. "Poison Lore and Chaucer's Pardoner," *Massachusetts Studies in English* 9, no. 1 (1983): 54–63.

Halverson, John. "Chaucer's Pardoner and the Progress of Criticism." *The Chaucer Review* 4 (1970): 184–202.

Hamilton, Marie P. "Death and Old Age in the Pardoner's Tale." *The Review of English Studies* n.s. 2 (1951): 49–55.

Howard, Donald R. *The Idea of* The Canterbury Tales. Berkeley and Los Angeles: University of California Press, 1976.

Huppé, Bernard F. *A Reading of* The Canterbury Tales. Albany: State University of New York Press, 1967.

Kellogg, Alfred L. "An Augustinian Interpretation of Chaucer's Pardoner." *Speculum* 26 (1951): 465–81.

Kellogg, Alfred L., and Louis A. Haselmayer. "Chaucer's Satire of the Pardoner." *PMLA* 66 (1951): 251–77.

Kittredge, George Lyman. *Chaucer and His Poetry.* Cambridge: Harvard University Press, 1915.

Knight, Stephen. "Chaucer's Pardoner in Performance." *Sydney Studies in English* 9 (1983–84): 21–36.

Lumiansky, R. M. *Of Sondry Folk.* Austin: University of Texas Press, 1955.

Miller, Robert P. "Chaucer's Pardoner, the Scriptural Eunuch, and the Pardoner's Tale." *Speculum* 30 (1955): 180–99.

Moisan, Thomas. "Shakespeare's Chaucerian Allegory: The Quest for Death in *Romeo and Juliet* and the Pardoner's Tale." In *Chaucerian Shakespeare: Adaptation and Transformation,* edited by E. Talbot Donaldson and Judith J. Kollmann, 131–49. Ann Arbor: Michigan Consortium for Medieval and Early Modern Studies, 1983.

Morgan, Gerald. "The Self-Revealing Tendencies of Chaucer's Pardoner." *The Modern Language Review* 71 (1976): 241–55.

Nichols, Robert E. "The Pardoner's Ale and Cake." *PMLA* 82 (1967): 498–504.

Nitecki, Alicia K. "The Convention of the Old Man's Lament in the Pardoner's Tale." *The Chaucer Review* 16 (1981): 76–84.

Olsen, Alexandra Hennessey. " 'They Shul Desiren to Dye, and Deeth Shal Flee Fro Hem': A Reconsideration of the Pardoner's Old Man." *Neuphilologische Mitteilungen* 84 (1983): 367–71.

Owen, Nancy. "The Pardoner's Introduction, Prologue, and Tale: Sermon and Fabliau." *Journal of English and Germanic Philology* 66 (1967): 541–49.

Owen, W. J. B. "The Old Man in the Pardoner's Tale." *The Review of English Studies* n.s. 2 (1951): 49–55.

Patterson, Lee W. "Chaucerian Confession: Penitential Literature and the Pardoner." *Medievalia et Humanistica* n.s. 7 (1976): 153–73.

Pearsall, Derek. "Chaucer's Pardoner: The Death of a Salesman." *The Chaucer Review* 17 (1983): 358–65.

Pittock, Malcolm. "The Pardoner's Tale and the Quest for Death." *Essays in Criticism* 24 (1974): 107–23.

Reiss, Edmund. "The Final Irony of the Pardoner's Tale." *College English* 25 (1964): 260–66.

Rhodes, James F. "Motivation in Chaucer's Pardoner's Tale: Winner Take Nothing." *The Chaucer Review* 17 (1982): 40–61.

Robertson, D. W., Jr. *A Preface to Chaucer.* Princeton, N. J.: Princeton University Press, 1962.

Rowland, Beryl. "Animal Imagery and the Pardoner's Abnormality." *Neophilologus* 48 (1964): 56–60.

————. "Chaucer's Idea of the Pardoner." *The Chaucer Review* 14 (1979): 140–54.

Ruggiers, Paul G. *The Art of* The Canterbury Tales. Madison: University of Wisconsin Press, 1965.

Schauber, Ellen, and Ellen Spolsky. "Conversational Noncooperation: The Case of Chaucer's Pardoner." *Language and Style* 16 (1983): 249–61.

Schoeck, Richard J., and Jerome Taylor, eds. *Chaucer Criticism, Volume I:* The Canterbury Tales. Notre Dame, Ind.: University of Notre Dame Press, 1960.

Sedgewick, G. G. "The Progress of Chaucer's Pardoner, 1880–1940." *Modern Language Quarterly* 1 (1940): 431–58.

Shain, Charles E. "Pulpit Rhetoric in Three Canterbury Tales." *MLN* 70 (1955): 235–45.

Spearing, A. C., ed. *The Pardoner's Prologue and Tale.* Cambridge: Cambridge University Press, 1965.

Steadman, John M. "Old Age and *Contemptus Mundi* in the Pardoner's Tale." *Medium Aevum* 33 (1964): 121–30.

Stevens, Martin, and Kathleen Falvey. "Substance, Accident, and Transformations: A Reading of the Pardoner's Tale." *The Chaucer Review* 17 (1982): 142–58.

Stockton, Eric. "The Deadliest Sin in the Pardoner's Tale." *Tennessee Studies in Literature* 6 (1961): 47–59.

Toole, William B. "Chaucer's Christian Irony: The Relationship of Character and Action in the Pardoner's Tale." *The Chaucer Review* 3 (1968): 37–43.

Tupper, Frederick. "The Pardoner's Tale." In *Sources and Analogues of Chaucer's* Canterbury Tales, edited by W. F. Bryan and Germaine Dempster, 415–38. New York: Humanities Press, 1958.

Wenzel, Siegfried. "Chaucer and the Language of Contemporary Preaching." *Studies in Philology* 73 (1976): 138–61.

Whittock, Trevor. *A Reading of* The Canterbury Tales. Cambridge: Cambridge University Press, 1968.

Acknowledgments

"The Narrative Art of the Pardoner's Tale" by Ian Bishop from *Medium Aevum* 36, no. 1 (1967), © 1967 by the Society for the Study of Mediaeval Languages and Literature. Reprinted by permission.

"The Pardoner's 'Jape' " by Penelope Curtis from *Critical Review* 11 (1968), © 1968 by Penelope Curtis. Reprinted by permission.

"The 'Floating' Fragment" (originally entitled "The Pardoner and the Parson") by Donald R. Howard from *The Idea of the* Canterbury Tales by Donald R. Howard, © 1976 by the Regents of the University of California. Reprinted by permission of the University of California Press.

" 'Modernizing' Chaucer" (originally entitled "The Pardoner and the Parson") by Donald R. Howard from *The Idea of the* Canterbury Tales by Donald R. Howard, © 1976 by the Regents of the University of California. Reprinted by permission of the University of California Press.

"Preaching and Avarice in the Pardoner's Tale" by Warren Ginsberg from *Mediaevalia* 2 (1976), © 1976 by the Center for Mediaeval and Early Renaissance Studies. Reprinted by permission of the Center for Mediaeval and Early Renaissance Studies, State University of New York at Binghamton.

" 'Synne Horrible': The Pardoner's Exegesis of His Tale, and Chaucer's" by H. Marshall Leicester, Jr., from *Acts of Interpretation: The Text in Its Contexts, 700–1600: Essays on Medieval and Renaissance Literature in Honor of E. Talbot Donaldson*, edited by Mary J. Carruthers and Elizabeth D. Kirk, © 1982 by Pilgrim Books. Reprinted by permission.

"The Pardoner's Homosexuality and How It Matters" by Monica E. McAlpine from *PMLA* 95, no. 1 (January 1980), © 1980 by the Modern Language Association of America. Reprinted by permission of the Modern Language Association of America.

"Sermon Structure in the Pardoner's Tale" by Robert P. Merrix from *The Chaucer Review* 17, no. 3 (1983), © 1983 by the Pennsylvania State University. Reprinted by permission of the Pennsylvania State University Press.

"The Pardoner and the Word of Death" by R. A. Shoaf from *Dante, Chaucer, and the Currency of the Word: Money, Images, and Reference in Late Medieval Poetry* by R. A. Shoaf, © 1983 by Pilgrim Books. Reprinted by permission.

Index

Absalom (Miller's Tale), 13
Achilles (*Iliad*), 5, 6
Alain de Lille, 67, 76
Aleyn (Reeve's Tale), 13
Allegory: in medieval sermons, 66; of Old Man, 20; of Pardoner, 101, 147, 150; and personification of Death, 14, 16–17, 52; throughout tale, 19–20, 52, 61–62, 79, 140; in tavern scene, 89–90; of the wine, 93–94. *See also* Imagery; Pardoner's Tale, typological elements in; Symbolism
Anselm, St., 129, 130
Apius (Physician's Tale), 45
Apothecary, 14, 15, 18, 93
Arcite (Knight's Tale), 143
Aretino, Pietro, 3
Aristophanes, 4
Aristotle, 4
Artes praedicandi, 63–64, 65, 126, 129, 131. *See also* Preaching
Astazius, 65
Auerbach, Erich, 34
Augustine, St., 46, 50, 62, 64, 65, 66, 67, 143–44
Austen, Jane, 4
Avarice: as chief sin in tale, 12–13, 15, 133–34; *cupiditas* as distinct from, 88, 133; as downfall of rioters, 12–13, 20, 51, 55; gloss of, 70; homiletic material on, 69–77; as motive of Physician, 44; oak tree as image of, 69; Old Man as sym-

bol of, 155; of the Pardoner, 44, 50, 97, 115–16, 119, 155; as theme in tale, 137–38

Bailly, Harry or Herry. *See* Host
Balzac, Honoré de, 3
Baudelaire, Charles, 3
Baugh, Albert, 108
Bede, The Venerable, 94, 129
Bible, 2, 109
Blake, William, 3–4, 7
Bloom, Leopold (*Ulysses*), 2, 4
Bloomfield, Morton, 134
Boccaccio, Giovanni, 2
Boniface, St., 126, 129
Boy (the Servant), 14, 16, 53, 54, 90
Brown, Carlton, 131
Browning, Robert, 4
Burke, Kenneth, 5
Byron, George Gordon, Lord, 4

Canon, 23, 29, 31
Canterbury Tales: Chaucer's use of sermon literature for, 125; Chaucer's use of typological methods in, 100–101; General Prologue to, 43–44, 45, 46, 104, 142–43, 154; importance of Pardoner to, 154; lack of speakers' self-consciousness in, 101; placement of Pardoner's Tale in, 46–47; Pardoner's and Physician's tales as fragment in, 43–47;

171